# JOEL SERRA'S

## MODERN SPANISH KITCHEN

### BY JOEL SERRA BEVIN

ROBINSON

# THIS IS A COOKBOOK ABOUT LIFE
# IN AND OUT
# OF THE KITCHEN

Joel Serra's Modern Spanish Kitchen is about being a rock star every day – in and out of the kitchen. It's a philosophy and lifestyle that demands you keep dreaming and, above all, keep cooking. It's not just about catching what you eat, but about hunting life, gorging on it and going back for seconds – when it comes to life, gluttony is never a sin.

It's also about cooking and living with an open heart because everything tastes better when it's prepared with love and shared with others.

And finally, it's about always expecting the unexpected. Life in and out of the kitchen is one big messy experiment and the best results come only to those who risk it all.

This book is a visual narrative that guides you through my own delicious chaos.

# THE KITCHEN DIDN'T TEACH ME HOW TO COOK
## IT TAUGHT ME
## HOW TO LIVE

(Im)perfection on the plate demands multiple messy experiments in the kitchen.

Recipe books are useful as a guide, but in the kitchen, always trust your instincts.

The most tedious kitchen tasks are fundamental for success on the plate.

Inspiration comes from experience, so cook everything and anything at least once.

The best dishes are often happened upon by accident, chance and serendipity.

Kitchen battle scars are worth it if you make your guests sigh with pleasure at the table.

Tricks and gadgets in the kitchen will cover up bad apples only for so long.

Every other chef is taken, so carry your own knife and stay authentic.

If it's just not your day, get out of the kitchen and order Chinese takeaway.

Cook happy because good vibes and plenty of lovin' are your *mise en place*.

Food always tastes better when shared, so pull up a seat and join the feast.

## STAY HUNGRY, MY FRIENDS

**JOEL SERRA BEVIN,** aka *Papa Serra Jr*, was born in New Zealand and grew up in Tasmania, Australia's southernmost island and quite literally the end of the world.

He passed eight years working as an economist in Melbourne, while on the weekends running a supper club out of his apartment, and also enjoying 15 minutes (more than enough) of fame on *MasterChef Australia*.

Realizing he preferred cracking nuts over crunching numbers, Joel left life as a consultant and moved to Barcelona where he founded Papa Serra Culinary Adventures (named after his Catalan great-grandfather). He launched a Barcelona rooftop supper club, collaborated on pop-up dining tours around the world, and hosted culinary adventures in all parts of Spain.

From there, Joel went on to lead the private chef and social dining movement around the world, convinced by the power of food to unite.

With personal heroes ranging from Hunter S. Thompson to Anthony Bourdain, Joel strives to create work that is original, entertaining and always delicious.

**ALDO CHACON** was born in Mexico City. Having travelled and lived around the world, he is never short of photographic inspiration, finding it in different faces, personalities, urban life and modern society.

He believes that everyone has a story to tell and it is his job to dig into personalities and share the secrets through his photos; he is a visual storyteller.

Growing up, food was always front and centre, and his childhood memories are filled with experiences in the kitchen and around the dinner table. With his love for portraits and urban style, Aldo combined his artistic experience with Joel's crazy ideas in what proved to be a truly original book.

# ABOUT
# THE AUTHORS

# WHO IS PAPA SERRA?

## SPANISH ROOTS

**PAPA SERRA** (my Catalan great-grandfather) was no chef, but he inspired me to seek out my cultural roots and represent them the only way I know how – on the plate.

Il started cooking out of necessity when my mother had a baking disaster the night before a school fair, forcing me to pull out a mixing bowl and embark on the first of many kitchen experiments.

Later, while working in a suit and tie, I realized I needed a creative release and started running a supper club (Global Gobbler) out of my apartment. I would invite guests to join multi-course tasting menus, during which I had a chance to share my passion for food and test my creations on a wider audience. Word spread and one night a national food critic turned up for dinner and published a review in *The Australian* newspaper. This public vote of confidence convinced me that dinner parties among total strangers had a future.

I then somehow found myself on the first season of *MasterChef Australia*, where I became famous more for cutting fingers than onions (I still have the bloody apron to this day). I made it through elimination after elimination before my time was up and I returned to a less dramatic but equally food-filled reality.

# CULINARY ADVENTURES

At the age of 24, I left Melbourne to pursue a dream that was blurry – I wanted to go to Barcelona, and studying (master's in Refugee Law) seemed like the perfect excuse. But somehow I ended up with sand between my textbooks and notes covered in red wine and crumbs, a good indication that my future was destined to be more about living a life surrounded by cookbooks than textbooks.

I still had career ambitions, so after grinding out a thesis, I moved to London for a good, sensible job. But Barcelona is a hard city to turn your back on, so I started writing recipes on Spanish food and, after a year of grey skies and in dire need of just one real tomato, I followed my stomach back to Barcelona; because we can always start again.

Having ceremonially burnt my suits and ties, I arrived in Barcelona, a year after leaving, wearing a chef's jacket and armed with a sharp knife. With these essentials, I immersed myself in the local food scene; Barcelona provided a banquet and I was gorging on it.

I wandered markets throwing my money at the old ladies selling briny razor clams and salty cured tuna, passed hours memorizing cookbooks from doyens of authentic Spanish chefs, such as Simone Ortega, as well as the most avant-garde genius of Ferran Adrià.

On the weekends I got back to nature: trekking in the mountains where I sought out wild herbs, green almonds and forest berries, and swimming with all manner of sea creatures up and down the Costa Brava. I also connected with my Catalan roots, the deep authenticity of which gave soul to my raw creativity.

But outside of my epicurean bubble, the reality of Barcelona's food scene washed over me in a greasy wave of shame. Bars served up token plates of predictable *pinchos* and stingy bowls of melancholic olives, while restaurants fooled all but a few with soggy pans of fluorescent yellow rice. It was the gastronomic killing fields.

With reckless abandon I decided to enter the fray and created Papa Serra Culinary Adventures: an immersive food experience that shared a new style of Spanish cooking and revealed the delicious underbelly of Barcelona's food scene.

I never planned to transform into Papa Serra Jr or write *Joel Serra's Modern Spanish Kitchen*; I simply went with my instincts (my stomach) and never stopped believing that there is no downside to creating food and love, which are basically the same thing.

# A COOKBOOK IS BORN

Crossing paths with Aldo over food, I immediately knew he was the photographer to help create my cookbook and we found a common creative groove. We spent several months plotting a truly original publication that would blend my recipes with his photography and showcase our creativity and uncontrollable passion for food and all the good stuff that goes with it.

With the recipes written and tested, we began the mammoth task of cooking and shooting almost 80 recipes. With both of us holding down demanding full-time jobs (myself as Head of EatWith Global Community and Aldo as an in-demand fashion photographer), we spent many weekends and late nights together in the kitchen, cooking, styling and shooting recipes over and over again.

But it wasn't just about the recipes; it was also about capturing our childlike enthusiasm for food, cooking and life, because 'life is too important to be taken seriously' (Oscar Wilde).

*Joel Serra's Modern Spanish Kitchen* is about the food, the story and the place. And there is no place like Barcelona. We created in and out of the kitchen, using the natural beauty and insane creativity that the city feeds you on every corner.

This book is not just a cookbook; it's about inspiring you to feast on life in all its delicious glory.

*All oven temperatures stated (in Celsius or Gas Mark) are for standard ovens and not for fan forced or convection ovens. Generally the temperature would be reduced by 20°C for a fan forced oven, but check your manufacturer's handbook for more specific instructions.*

*This book gives metric measurements throughout. If you prefer to use imperial or US measurements, please use these conversions.*

| Imperial | Metric | American |
|----------|--------|----------|
| ½ fl oz | 15ml | 1 tablespoon |
| 1 fl oz | 30ml | ⅛ cup |
| 2 fl oz | 60ml | ¼ cup |
| 4 fl oz | 120ml | ½ cup |
| 8 fl oz | 240ml | 1 cup |
| 16 fl oz | 480ml | 1 pint |
| | | |
| 4oz | 100g | |
| 7oz | 200g | |
| 10oz | 300g | |
| 13oz | 400g | |
| 1lb | 500g | |

# SAUCES AND STOCKS [12]

ALLIOLI / ROMESCO / SALSA VERDE / CHICKEN CALDO / SEAFOOD FUMET

# TAPAS [28]

SPICED ALMONDS / BAKED GOATS' CHEESE / PIMIENTOS DE PADRÓN / MANCHEGO / PÀ AMB TOMÀQUET / SON-IN-LAW EGGS / CHORIZO / ARTICHOKE BUNYOLS / CLAMS / MELÓN WITH JAMÓN / OLIVES / CHICKPEAS / BANDERILLA / MUSHROOMS / MEATBALLS / CALÇOTS / PIQUILLO PEPPERS / TORTILLA

# SOUPS [70]

AJO BLANCO / GREEN GAZPACHO / GAZPACHUELO / ROMESCO DE PEIX

# VEGETABLES [78]

GREEN SALAD / AUBERGINES / CARROTS / TOMATOES / PUMPKIN / XATÓ / FENNEL / BEETROOT / COURGETTE / COLESLAW / CAULIFLOWER / POTATOES / ARTICHOKES / RUSSIAN SALAD

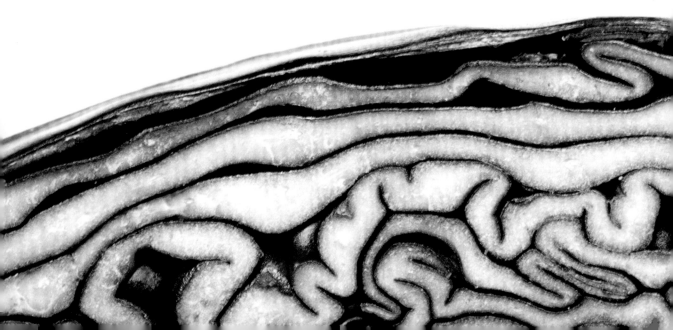

# RECIPES

## FROM THE SEA 112
PULPO A LA GALLEGA / SARDINES / FIDEUÀ / TROUT / SALMON / BABY SQUID / ESCABECHE /
SCALLOPS / SAFFRON FISH / ESQUEIXADA / MUSSELS / BONITO

## FROM THE LAND 144
LAMB SHANKS / CHICKEN IN SHERRY VINEGAR / LENTILS / RABBIT / SAFFRON CHICKEN

## SWEETS 158
TURRÓN ICE CREAM / TORTA DE SANTIAGO / WATERMELON GAZPACHO / PEARS / FIGS /
ALMENDRINA CHEESECAKE / MEMBRILLO / SORBET / LECHE MERENGADA /
CHOCOLATE MOUSSE

## DRINKS 188
CAFÉ CON HIELO / HORCHATA / VICHY / CAVA / CIDER / CLARA / SANGRIA /
SPANISH HOT CHOCOLATE / VERMOUTH

All recipes are designed
for four people, but hunger
triggers volatile emotions
so feel free to adapt for
maximum satisfaction.

# SAUCES
## AND STOCKS

# YOU KNOW YOU'VE MET THE ONE WHEN YOU CAN EAT ALLIOLI AND KISS ON THE SAME NIGHT

My ten-year-old self could never forget Papa Serra's blow-your-head-off garlicky allioli and, since then, many a passionate moment in my life has suffered. No matter how charming one tries to be, one-liners said while chewing gum and turning your head to the side are never going to win hearts. But a solid session with the mortar and pestle heals all regrets of romantic liaisons that might have been.

Allioli is the stuff fried potatoes lust over, it is the ingredient charred squid craves, and the magic that makes fideuá truly glorious.

Growing up literally on the other side of the world in Australia, where industrial margarine and unsalted butter held sway, it was only by smuggling in vast quantities of thick Spanish olive oil that I was able to replicate this rustic sauce and keep the flavour of Spain in my heart, and on my breath.

# ALLIOLI

**15 MIN**

## Ingredients

2 garlic cloves, crushed
120ml extra-virgin olive oil
Juice of ¼ lemon
Salt

## Method

Using a mortar and pestle, crush the garlic cloves with a generous pinch of salt to form a smooth paste. Then, drizzle in the olive oil little by little, mixing furiously to incorporate the oil as you go (careful not to add too much, as this will cause the sauce to separate). Add oil until a thick creamy white sauce forms – if the pestle can stand up on its own, you're done.

Thankfully there are no exacts – no two batches of allioli will ever be the same. This is Mediterranean cooking at its most basic and its best.

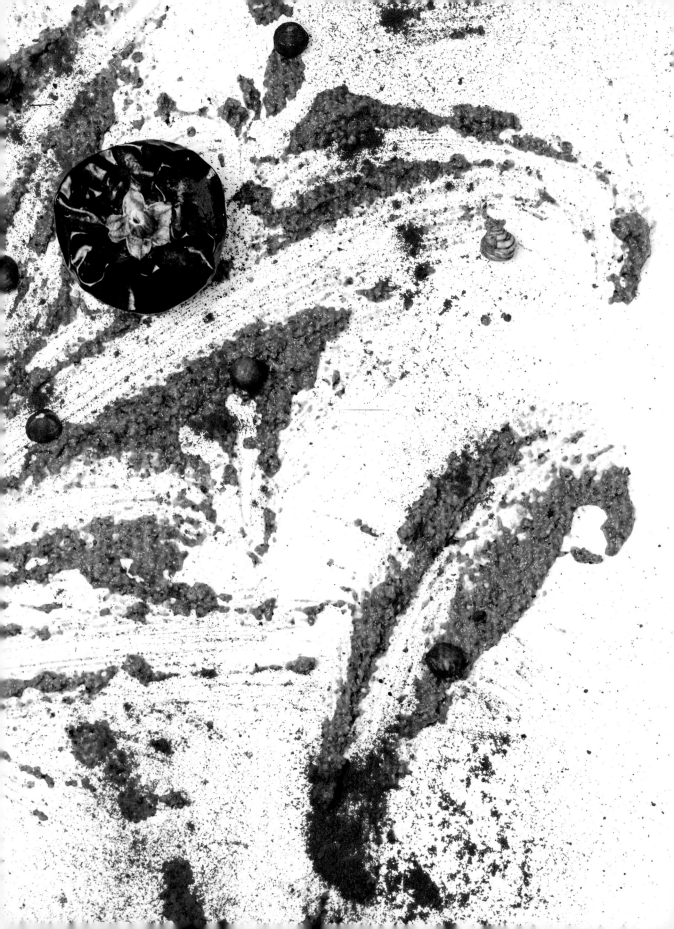

# HEINZ GAVE THE WORLD KETCHUP, THE ROMANS GAVE US ROMESCO

## GAME OVER.

There is something special about Tarragona. It is the birthplace of not only allioli, but also romesco, Spain's most quintessential sauce. Renowned Catalan journalist Josep Pla wrote that 'I don't think there are many cities in the world that have a sauce of their own.' Tarragona was obviously a Roman emulsification hub.

Traditionally used to flavour soups and stews, romesco was first introduced to me as a dip for potato chips in a cheap and cheerful *chiringuito* in Murcia. Pairing this noble sauce with the humble potato seems to be a nice way of linking the Romans with the sunny simplicity of the Costa Brava.

# ROMESCO

**20–25 MIN**

## Ingredients

2 ripe tomatoes, halved

1 red pepper, halved and deseeded

1 whole bulb of garlic, sliced in half crossways, unpeeled, plus 1 clove, peeled

1 tsp fresh or dried thyme leaves

4 tbsp olive oil, plus extra for blending

1 dried nyora pepper or ancho chilli, seeds removed and soaked in water

1 tbsp smoked paprika

2 tbsp chopped flat-leaf parsley leaves

3 tbsp red wine vinegar

Dry red wine, to taste

Slices of crusty bread, as needed

75g unblanched almonds, skin on

75g hazelnuts

Salt and cracked black pepper

## Method

Preheat the oven to 200°C/Gas Mark 6. Lay the tomatoes and red pepper halves, skin side up, on a tray, along with the garlic halves. Sprinkle over with the thyme and olive oil, and season with salt and cracked pepper. Place in the oven and roast for 20 minutes until the pepper skins begin to blacken, then remove from the oven and cover with foil. Once cool, peel away the pepper skins and discard, then place the pepper flesh and tomatoes into a blender along with the roasted garlic cloves with skin still on, soaked nyora pepper or ancho chilli, smoked paprika, parsley, the clove of raw garlic, red wine vinegar, another splash of oil, a slice of crusty bread and a splash of red wine. Set aside.

Bring a small pan of water to the boil. Once boiling, tip in the almonds and blanch for 2 minutes. Drain, then refresh in cold water. Squeeze the nuts out of their skins, discard the skins and place on a baking tray with the hazelnuts and roast until golden and crunchy. Rub the hazelnuts together to remove skins, then add both nuts to the blender. Whizz the ingredients until smooth, then review the consistency, adding another hunk of bread if the sauce needs thickening or a splash of red wine if it needs thinning, then adjust the seasoning with additional salt, oil and vinegar. Taste, taste, taste!

Store in the fridge where it will keep for up to a week, although I'm betting it won't last more than a few days.

Democracy and a green sauce are the two tenets of any great nation. The French add mayonnaise and tarragon to create their verte, the Canary Islands rely on coriander for the peppy mojo; there is Argentina's chimichurri laden with oregano and dried chilli, the Italians flavour their pesto with basil, pine nuts and Reggiano; Mexicans turn up the heat with green tomatillos and jalapeños, while Germany has grüne sose, rich with sour cream, yogurt and chives. Spain is missing a nationally recognized one, so I combine sherry vinegar, lemon, almonds and anchovies with parsley and rosemary to create a thick, zesty sauce that lifts plates of potatoes, chicken wings, black lentils and lamb cutlets to hero status. You can choose your leader (or so they say), but I cast my ballot with green sauce in mind.

# SPANISH
# SALSA VERDE

**15 MIN**

### Ingredients

40g unblanched almonds

1 tsp fennel seeds

Juice and zest of 1 lemon

2 tbsp fresh rosemary

2 garlic cloves, peeled

5 anchovy fillets, finely chopped

2 tbsp fresh mint leaves

4 tbsp chopped flat-leaf parsley leaves

2 tbsp capers, finely chopped

3 tbsp sherry vinegar, plus extra to taste

4 tbsp extra-virgin olive oil, plus extra to taste

Salt and cracked black pepper

### Method

Toast the almonds under a hot grill for 5–10 minutes until beginning to darken, then remove them and set aside to cool. Once cooled, chop roughly.

Toast the fennel seeds the same way for 1 minute, then tip the seeds into a mortar along with the lemon zest, rosemary and garlic. Use the pestle to grind the mixture into a fragrant paste. Tip the paste into a blender along with the anchovies, mint, parsley, capers, sherry vinegar and half the oil. Whizz until a thick sauce forms. Add additional oil and whizz again until the sauce is smooth and glossy. Taste and adjust the seasoning with additional vinegar, oil, salt or pepper, then store in the fridge where it will keep for up to a week.

Although I left Spain for London in 2011, my heart and, more importantly, my stomach missed the flight. On touchdown in England, I sought out the narcotically priced saffron, I closed my eyes while downing glasses of Rioja as it drizzled outside, and I made it a rule to never eat before 9pm. What made life bearable was the Madrileña with whom I shared an apartment. María José was the Spanish sunshine that made me forget for a moment that finding a truly ripe tomato was a pipedream. She was wise and worldly like my mother, and cooked like her, too. I remember her amazing salads, dressed with lemon juice, capers, olive oil and sherry vinegar; her baguettes layered with vacuum-packed *jamón* that arrived via courier from Madrid every month; and her hearty soups, packed with chickpeas, chunks of carrot, celery, potato and fatty cuts of pork. It was close to the middle of winter when we decided to make *arroz caldoso* together. Rice might be an accompaniment elsewhere around the world, but it is the main game in Spain. Gently frying onions in olive oil with salt and smoked paprika set up the dish for a deep hearty bone-warming stock that the grains gratefully soak up until they become plump and juicy pearls. Peasants know how to eat – that much is for sure.

# CHICKEN CALDO    120 MIN

## Ingredients

Extra-virgin olive oil

1 onion, diced

1 leek, cleaned and roughly chopped

2 carrots, cleaned and roughly chopped

1 whole chicken carcass (ask your butcher for one or simply take the breasts and
   thighs off a whole chicken and hack it into rough pieces)

A handful of fresh flat-leaf parsley (stalks and all)

4 bay leaves

A bunch of thyme

5 black peppercorns

Peel of 1 lemon

½ litre white wine

A big pinch of salt

## Method

Drizzle a little oil into a large heavy-bottomed saucepan and add all the vegetables. Gently sauté them over a medium heat until the vegetables are beginning to soften. Add the chicken carcass along with the parsley, bay leaves, thyme, peppercorns and lemon peel and continue to fry for another 10 minutes (add more oil as needed). Add the wine and 2 litres of water, bring to the boil, then reduce the heat and simmer gently for at least 90 minutes until the smell of chicken broth wafts through the house. Strain the liquid and set aside to cool. The caldo will keep for a week in the fridge. You can use it as the stock for any dishes demanding a deep, hearty base.

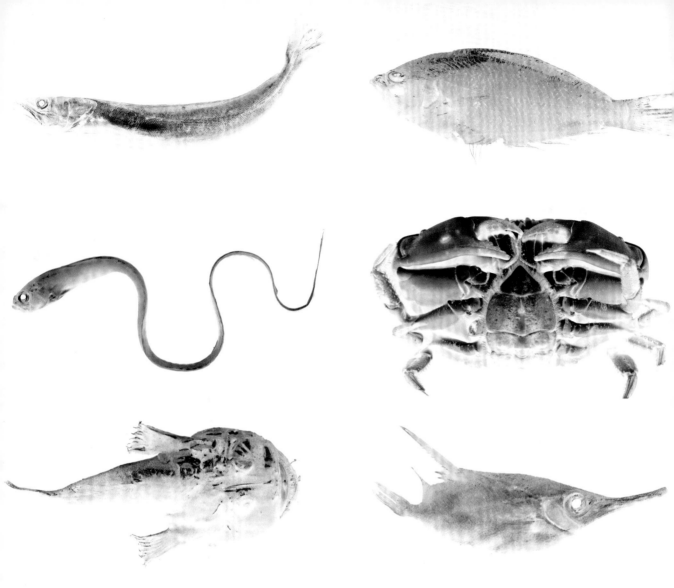

For most of the world, fish stock comes in cubes and cartons, but in Spain, *fumet* comes from the heads and tails of the sea. Watching my adopted godmother María-Angeles prepare *fumet* remains a culinary highlight that flashes back every time I feel like lazily turning to the packaged version. First, she warmed olive oil in a cast-iron pot, then she added onions, leeks, carrots and bay leaves and fried them until the vegetables started to soften, then she threw in all manner of sea creatures – prawn heads, baby crabs, monkfish tails, empty mussel shells and, perhaps most impressive, lobster claws, which every gourmet has hiding in the back of their fridge. With a flourish, she pitched in the final seasoning (lemon, white peppercorns and parsley), before covering with water and wine and bringing the pot to a simmer. When strained two hours later, the liquid could have easily passed as a soup, but instead it formed the base of an *arroz de sepia* (squid rice) that left each grain bursting with the flavour of the ocean. When the pace of life allows, I spend hours making *fumet*. In today's hyper-connected world where life hacks are badges of honour, setting aside the time to make *fumet* is priceless. It's a reward I treat myself to when I need to connect with something deeper and cook with a reference to the older and wiser people that I've met along the way.

# SEA CREATURES
## MAKE FOR GREAT SWIMMING PARTNERS AND EVEN BETTER COMPANIONS IN THE KITCHEN

# SEAFOOD FUMET 75 MIN

## Ingredients

Extra-virgin olive oil
1 brown onion, diced
3 stalks celery, roughly chopped
2 carrots, roughly chopped
1kg leftover empty mussel or clam shells
1kg leftover spines and heads of any white fish
5 handfuls of fresh parsley, stalks and all
4 bay leaves
5 whole white peppercorns
Peel of 1 lemon
½ litre of white wine

## Method

Heat some oil in a large heavy-based saucepan, then add the onion, celery and carrots and fry over medium heat until the vegetables begin to soften. Add all the seafood and fry for a further 5 minutes until well coated in oil. Next, add the parsley, bay leaves, peppercorns and lemon peel and fry for another 5 minutes. Add the wine and 2 litres of water and simmer gently for at least 1 hour, then strain through a sieve and set aside to cool. Store in the fridge and use it within a week, or freeze it in several batches for use throughout the year.

**TAPAS**

Outside of the sunny Mediterranean bubble that Spain basks in, beers tend to come in larger glasses, which often require two hands to raise to one's lips. I may eat quickly but when it comes to beer, I prefer to sip than skull, despite the inevitable ridicule. The Spanish *caña* (a draught beer) is brewed perfection. Measuring about half a pint, a *caña* remains ice-cold through to the last gulp, even for miserable drinkers like me. After a few hours responsibly enjoying my *cañas* of simple lager, I find myself driven to seek out handfuls of salty snacks. In Spain this means almonds – toasted, then gently fried in olive oil and dusted with salt and spices. In Malaga street vendors on every corner sell them in cones as the obvious evening antidote for those still struggling to adjust to 10pm dinner times. Most vendors hit them with the sweet smoky flavour of pimentón, which I like to combine with Moorish cinnamon and the fresh bite of fennel seeds. But why not create your own blend of spices (cumin, turmeric, nutmeg) for the perfect crunch. And don't forget plentiful fist-sized beers as you reflect on the joys of Mediterranean life.

# SPICED ALMONDS

**15 MIN**

### Ingredients
75g unblanched almonds
1 tbsp fennel seeds
1 tbsp pimentón (smoky paprika)
½ tsp cinnamon
1 tsp extra-virgin olive oil
Salt and cracked black pepper

### Method
Preheat the oven to 180°C/Gas Mark 4. Bring a small pan of water to the boil, then add the almonds and blanch them for 1 minute. Drain them and then refresh under cold running water. Squeeze each almond to remove the skins. In a mortar and pestle, grind the fennel seeds with the pimentón, cinnamon and a generous pinch of salt until you have a fine powder. Place the peeled almonds in a small bowl, drizzle over the oil, then stir to coat the nuts in the oil. Place the nuts on a baking tray and sprinkle over the ground spices. Roast the coated nuts in the hot oven for 10 minutes until the almonds are beginning to turn golden, then remove from the oven and set aside to cool and gain their crunch. Store the nuts in an airtight jar for up to two weeks and serve as the ultimate bar snack.

# MELTED CHEESE SHOULD BE CLASSIFIED AS A NARCOTIC

There is no doubt melted cheese deserves its cult-like status. Think about the addictive nature of some of its best iterations: margherita pizzas topped with fresh mozzarella in Naples, potatoes with raclette cheese in the Swiss Alps or a croque monsieur rich with brie in Paris. Growing up, my favourite cheesy incarnation involved wedges of salty Cheddar arranged on hunks of my father's homemade bread and grilled until bubbling and golden, then roughly cut in two before being dipped in supermarket-brand ketchup and devoured in a matter of bites. Like cheese, it seems I've matured. Goats' cheese stays true to the mountain herbs on which these four-legged creatures feast. Pair it with tomato and rosemary jam and lather the messy concoction on a fresh baguette for a truly satisfying melting moment. Nothing will ever replace the original, enjoyed with after-school cartoons, but this version remains a guilty pleasure of which the glutton can be proud.

# BAKED
# GOATS' CHEESE
## WITH TOMATO AND ROSEMARY SYRUP

**45 MIN**

### Ingredients

10 tomatoes

Juice of 1 lemon

1 green apple (Granny Smith is ideal), peeled, cored and diced

3 tbsp brown sugar

120ml white wine

2 rosemary sprigs

3 tbsp sherry vinegar

65g walnuts

A big round of soft goats' cheese (*rulo de cabra* in Spain)

A handful of flat-leaf parsley, finely chopped

### Method

Heat the grill to medium. Bring a large pan of water to the boil. Drop the tomatoes into the water for 1 minute, then drain them and refresh in a bowl of iced water. One by one remove the tomatoes from the water and squeeze them out of their skins. Discard the skins, cut into wedges, remove the seeds and transfer them to a large saucepan. Add the lemon juice, diced apples, sugar, white wine and 1 sprig of rosemary. Place the pan over a low heat for 20 minutes, until the tomatoes have broken down and the apples are beginning to caramelize. Add the sherry vinegar and reduce for 10 minutes until it thickens. When it is like a thick sauce, remove from heat. Press the mixture through a sieve, discard the pulp and set the syrup aside.

Preheat the oven to 180°C/Gas Mark 4. Spread the walnuts on a baking tray and roast for 5 minutes until beginning to turn golden, then remove them and set aside to cool. Crush the walnuts in your hands and sprinkle on a baking tray. Set the cheese round on top of the walnuts and place under the grill for 10 minutes or until the cheese begins to turn golden and melt. Carefully transfer the cheese to a serving plate, drizzle some tomato syrup over the cheese and sprinkle with chopped parsley. Serve with crusty bread to mop up the pool of magical melted pleasure.

Spain gets hot, but Spanish food not so much. The fresh and zesty Mediterranean fills your mouth with flavour, but doesn't make your lips tingle. You'll soon find yourself heaping chilli flakes into pots of rice, adding fresh green chilli to gazpacho and squirting sriracha over crispy fried potatoes. This was until I discovered the *pimiento de Padrón*, a Galician speciality that is as obligatory a tapa as the Spanish tortilla (and much more interesting). One in ten of these salty green pockets are filled with searing heat (by Spanish standards), while the rest are sweet and savoury. No matter how many times I've been stung by the *Padrón*, I'm a sucker for this tasty game of Russian roulette, and anyone missing some heat on their plates is advised to spin the barrel.

# STUFFED PIMIENTOS DE PADRÓN

**10 MIN**

### Ingredients

300g pimientos de Padrón

100g manchego cheese, cut into small wedges

70g almonds (as many as needed to fill the pimientos), blanched and toasted

4 tbsp extra-virgin olive oil

A generous pinch of sea salt flakes

### Method

Simply cut a slit on the pepper and slide in a small slice of the manchego and a toasted almond. Pour the olive oil into a deep pan, then once bubbling, tip in the peppers (being careful not to overcrowd the pan). Fry and shake a few times until beginning to blister and blacken, then remove from the oil and set aside to drain on kitchen paper. Season with sea salt flakes and serve hot in every sense of the word.

Cheese for breakfast makes a lot of sense to me; indeed, some would say it has a place at every meal. While the salty sharpness can be jarring so early in the morning, my month in Moscow proved this to be a challenge I could easily overcome.

On a business trip studying the city's urban policies, long days and nights made breakfast literally the most important meal of the day. The hotel put on a morning buffet that was, quite frankly, obscene in its scale and scope. They allowed me to choose from four types of soft cheese and eight hard varieties, all set up for pairing with the six types of honey that ringed the dairy tabernacle. A token piece of fruit made way for twenty-four combinations of what turned out to be the only meal I needed in order to survive for the rest of the day and enjoy guaranteed cheese dreams through the night (they are a thing – Google it). Try combining the earthy flavours of coffee beans and rosemary, the aniseed flavour of fennel seed, and the tangy lemon aromas of coriander and cumin seeds, all packed and served neatly in the bitter crunchy vessel of endive leaves. Good Manchego (pure sheep's milk, if possible) and dark untreated chestnut, rosemary or thyme honey will see your dreams filled with visions of this umamic ecstasy.

# MANCHEGO
## WITH HONEY, NUTS, HERBS AND SPICES

**5 MIN**

### Ingredients
3–4 whole endive (green or purple)
300g Manchego cheese (there is no substitute!)
2 tbsp of raw honey

### Method
Separate the endive leaves and lay them on a dish. Fill each leaf with slices of Manchego and drizzle over with honey. Top each with the spices, herbs, zest and nuts, choosing whatever flavour combination feels right. To this day, my favourite remains freshly ground coffee, orange zest, pink peppercorns and rosemary.

### Options for the topping:
1 tsp each coriander, fennel and
    cumin seeds, toasted
1 tbsp fresh rosemary, finely
    chopped
1 tbsp freshly ground coffee powder
Zest of 1 orange
Zest of 1 lemon
75g walnuts, toasted
75g almonds, toasted
75g hazelnuts, toasted
2 tsp pink peppercorns
A generous pinch of Maldon sea salt

# THE ITALIANS RUB WITH GARLIC, THE SPANISH WITH TOMATOES WELCOME TO THE FAMILY

Since the beginning of the 20th century, Catalonia has been fighting for its independence from Spain, and at the time of writing, the constitutional challenges were taking place. Despite Catalan blood pulsing through my veins, I have always believed in a more connected world, and my faith in this respect remains unbroken. Besides, I feel like there is something more important to fight for in Spain: the Catalan *pà amb tomàquet*. Something as simple as bread with tomato should be mastered and shared proudly with a world bored of bland bread rolls and pats of butter. The formula seems straightforward: cut a crusty baguette lengthways, lightly toast (or not), rub with garlic (or not), squeeze and rub fresh tomato across the bread, then drizzle with oil and season with salt – it's basic. So, why do restaurants around the world still baulk at the idea of replacing French and Italian traditions with this Spanish interpretation?

While growing up in Australia, my mother made this Spanish gastronomic tradition an enduring reminder of my roots, and set me on a life of requesting olive oil with every slice of bread. Parisian waiters could barely contain their contempt! As an ambassador for Spanish cuisine, my cause is to unite the world around this Spanish tradition and prove that breaking bread is a way to bring people together, but only if it's done with tomato and oil.

# PÀ AMB TOMÀQUET 5–10 MIN

## Ingredients

1 baguette (rustic and chewy), sliced in half lengthways

1 garlic clove, peeled and halved

4 very ripe tomatoes (such as ramellet)

Olive oil

Salt

And if you feel you need more culinary adventures …

A small chunk of mojama (salt-cured tuna, which should be available in delicatessens or online)

4 slices of jamón (Ibérico, if possible)

A wedge of Manchego cheese (or another semi-hard goats' cheese)

½ ripe avocado

8 white anchovies

½ lemon

## Method

Heat the grill to high and toast the baguette halves (cut-side up) until beginning to turn golden. Rub the halved garlic clove over the cut sides of the toasted baguette halves. Slice the tomatoes crossways, then rub over the toasted baguette until all the juice and seeds have been squeezed out. Drizzle the baguettes with olive oil, then season with a pinch of salt. Master this basic version and then you can start thinking about going crazy – top with jamón, shaved Manchego, microplaned mojama, avocado and salty white anchovies. But for me, the original will always be the best.

It's impossible to ignore a dish with origins that revolve around protective mothers and threats to potential sons-in-laws' appendages. Originating in Thailand and traditionally topped with a tamarind-flavoured sweet-and-sour caramel, I have given eggs the Iberian treatment, layering the sweet smokiness of paprika with the herbaceous strength of bay leaves to create a deep caramel that stands up to the richness of deep-fried eggs. Mothers-in-law should generally be feared, but the prize, whether it be these eggs or their daughters, is surely worth all manner of pain.

# SPANISH SON-in-LAW EGGS
## WITH CHORIZO AND PAPRIKA CARAMEL

**60 MIN**

### Ingredients

1 brown onion, finely chopped

1 garlic clove, finely chopped

5cm chorizo, finely chopped

3 bay leaves

4 tomatoes, diced

100g brown sugar

120ml red wine vinegar

3 tbsp sweet paprika

3 tbsp smoked paprika

4 eggs

60g of flour

30g dried breadcrumbs

2 egg yolks, beaten

Sunflower oil for deep-frying

Salt

### Method

Add a glug of olive oil to a medium saucepan over a high heat. When the oil is hot, reduce the heat to low and add the onion, garlic, chorizo and bay leaves, season with salt and fry over a low heat for 10 minutes until caramelized. Add the diced tomato, brown sugar, red wine vinegar, sweet and smoked paprika and continue to fry for another 10 minutes, until the tomatoes have broken down and the liquid is beginning to thicken and turn glossy. Strain the mixture through a sieve, then return to the saucepan and simmer for a further 10 minutes, until the mixture has reduced to a caramel, then set aside.

Place the eggs in a small pan and add enough cold water to cover them. Bring the water to a boil, then remove the pan from the heat and let the eggs sit in the hot water for 6 minutes. Remove the eggs with a slotted spoon and peel them immediately. Place the flour, breadcrumbs and egg yolks in separate bowls. Fill a deep pan with sunflower oil and heat the oil to 150–200°C. Carefully coat each egg in yolk, then in flour, then return to the yolk and finally coat in breadcrumbs. Add eggs one at a time to the hot oil and deep-fry for 5 minutes until golden and crispy, then set aside on kitchen paper and repeat for the remaining eggs. Drizzle the caramel over the eggs and serve as a sure-fire way to win over any potential mother-in-law and her daughter.

If I'm eating charcuterie, I'm eating chorizo. It has a sweet meatiness that Italian salamis lack and a smoky spice that I miss in the fatty northern European versions. Every corner of Spain interprets chorizo differently, but it was in a green park on the outskirts of London that I first tasted this piggy delicacy. My language-exchange partner made sure our meet-ups always had a culinary base. From Madrid, she lugged suitcases packed to bursting with cartons of Orlando *tomate frito*, containers of chocolatey Cola Cao and thick stumps of chorizo. We chose Hampstead Heath as a worthy location to savour the bounty, and while I filled chipped cups with pricey imported Rioja, my friend carefully drizzled soft white rolls with olive oil before stuffing them with thick slices of chorizo. It was just another sandwich, but it kept my Spanish dream alive.

These days I am surrounded by markets selling chorizo and I like to cut the richness of the meat with crisp apple. The combination reminds me of my now daily scene where the weathered local elders dip their thick leathery bodies into Barceloneta's refreshing Mediterranean every morning. Yes, life imitates food.

# CHORIZO
## BRAISED IN CIDER WITH FRESH APPLE   20 MIN

### Ingredients
Extra-virgin olive oil
400g chorizo, sliced diagonally into 2cm rounds
200ml cider
1 tart dessert apple (such as Granny Smith)
Juice of 1 lemon
1 tsp sweet paprika
Crusty bread, to serve

### Method
Heat a glug of oil in a frying pan, then add the chorizo rounds and fry until starting to caramelize. Add the cider and coat the chorizo, then reduce the heat and leave until the liquid has evaporated. Remove from the heat.

Slice the apple into thin wedges, then dress with the lemon juice and set aside. Arrange the apple on a serving dish and top with the chorizo, then dust with paprika and serve with crusty bread.

For the uninitiated, eating artichokes is a complex exercise. When I took to my virgin artichoke, grilled and golden, there were no instructions guiding me to avoid the tough, inedible outer leaves and the furry choke. And so by the time I arrived at the sweet and savoury heart, I was all but defeated, mouth aching from masticating the outer roughage of this mysterious vegetable. My sister used to compare me to one, remarking with her trademark blunt love that likeability requires hard work. She continued to liken my older sister to a graceful bulb of fennel, my father a moreish sweet potato and my mother to an eccentric, bright pineapple. If you use as many adjectives to describe food as you do people, you'll quickly realize that every family has an artichoke.

# ARTICHOKE
## BUNYOLS WITH ROMESCO

**40 MIN**

### Ingredients

10 whole artichokes (if out of season, use frozen or
    tinned artichoke hearts)
Zest and juice of 1 lemon
Extra-virgin olive oil
1 garlic clove
1 bay leaf
4 thyme sprigs, plus extra leaves for sprinkling

120ml white wine
1 egg, beaten
100g mató (or ricotta)
60g dried breadcrumbs
Sunflower oil, for deep-frying
8 tbsp romesco (see page 21)
Salt and cracked black pepper

### Method

Preheat the grill to high. Bring a large pot of water to the boil. If you're using fresh artichokes, trim off the tips and remove the outer leaves, then cut the artichokes in half and scoop out the hairy choke. Slice the artichokes into segments and dress them with lemon juice and olive oil. Heat a few glugs of oil in a pan, then add the garlic, artichoke segments, thyme sprigs and bay leaf, and fry for 10 minutes until the garlic is beginning to caramelize. Add the wine and lower the heat, then simmer for 15 minutes until the liquid has reduced. Once all the liquid has fully evaporated, remove from the heat and remove the bay leaf, then blend the artichokes until smooth. Set aside.

In a large bowl, add the beaten egg and mató and combine until smooth. Add the mashed artichokes and lemon zest, and season with salt and black pepper combine well. Mix breadcrumbs with the extra thyme leaves and a pinch of salt to form a crumb then scoop in hunks of bunyol (artichoke) mixture and coat well. Heat the sunflower oil in a deep frying pan until sizzling hot and carefully add the bunyols, frying them for 10 minutes until golden brown and crunchy. Remove and then set aside to drain on kitchen paper. Serve hot with a bowl of romesco and chew your way to deep-fried heaven.

I will only ever associate this dish with a magical tapas bar in Granada called Los Diamantes (The Diamonds). After a day of marvelling at the Alhambra and quenching my thirst with glasses of *claras* (the Spanish shandy) and iced *tinto de verano* (summer red wine), my father, sister and I sat outside a random tapas bar where we spent the remainder of our night. Being Granada, the tapas matched our steady stream of drinks and were on the house – garlic prawns, *pimientos de padrón*, fried aubergine, hunks of chorizo, chicken wings in sherry – and then a sizzling plate of clams basted in a sauce of garlic, parsley and thick golden olive oil. Whenever I see these baby molluscs at the fish market, I forget what I had on my list and can't help but smile at what remains one of my most vivid food memories.

# CLAMS
## IN SAFFRON BUTTER

### Ingredients

2 garlic gloves
A pinch of saffron
2 tbsp flat-leaf parsley
Zest and juice of 1 lemon
Extra-virgin olive oil
500g clams, cleaned and rinsed
A knob of butter
Salt

### Method

Preheat the oven to 180°C/Gas Mark 4. Using a mortar and pestle, grind the garlic with the saffron, parsley and lemon zest. Season with salt and add olive oil a little at a time until you reach a pesto-like consistency.

Heat a good glug of oil in a large flying pan or saucepan over a low heat. Add the garlic mixture and slowly fry until the mixture begins to soften. Add the clams with another splash of olive oil and the butter, then toss them over the heat for a few minutes, until the clams have opened. Serve with crusty bread to mop up the briny juice. Best enjoyed in the late-night heat of Andalusia, at a certain bar that luckily remains a 'diamond in the rough' within Granada's narrow, winding streets.

These days we might parody 1980s dinner parties, but among the terrines, trifles, meatloaf and mocktails, the combination of melon with ham is one plate I'll stand by.

The Italian version uses cantaloupe melon and prosciutto; throughout Spain you'll find the lime-green sharlyn melon dressed with jamón. When I was in Andalusia, I used to start the day with a big chunk of melon, some fresh cheese and paper-thin slices of jamón. I'd sit with my breakfast in the morning sun with a paper that doubled as a napkin (depending on which section I was reading). At the peak of the season, you can get melons for less than 1 euro per kilo, making financial and gastronomic sense.

# MELÓN with JAMÓN and FRESH CHEESE FOAM

**10 MIN**

## Ingredients

½ Spanish sharlyn melon (or whatever local seasonal melon is
    available), skin removed, flesh chopped into bite-sized chunks
Juice of ½ lemon
100g queso fresco

30ml single cream
A handful of fresh basil leaves, roughly
    torn
5 jamón slices
1 tsp freshly ground coffee

## Method

Toss the melon chunks in the lemon juice and set aside. Use a hand blender to blend the queso fresco with the cream, until smooth. Lay a torn basil leaf on each segment of melon and top with a spoon of the queso fresco mixture, then drape a slice of jamón over the top. Serve sprinkled with coffee grounds and the remaining torn basil.

Olives – as close as a vegetable will ever come to joining the charcuterie board – are Mediterranean fundamentals and Spain produces some of the best. Salty, sweet and bitter, no Spanish table is complete without a bowl of these black and green gems. I love the fluorescent green Campo Real, the bitter Caspe and the tiny Arbequina (the source of every real Spanish olive oil), and of course the meaty black Morta. Curing olives carried an appeal I couldn't resist after moving into a Melbourne neighbourhood filled with Greek and Italian second-generation migrants. Their tomatoes competed with thick bushes of basil and shiny purple aubergines, and above them all towered weighty olive trees, from which thousands of the black and green berries would fall every summer. Making do with what had fallen, and guiltily stripping several branches (I have made good with my conscience to justify my ongoing urban foraging), I found myself heaving a T-shirt-full back home, whereupon I began to fill my modest ground-floor apartment with jars of olives, curing with lemon peel, chilli, garlic, rosemary and coriander seeds. I nervously shared the results with my suspicious neighbours and was congratulated with a grudging smile and shake of the head at this brazen generosity that made good on the earlier crime.

# HOME-CURED OLIVES

**Ingredients**
150g sea salt
1kg olives
Extra-virgin olive oil

**Method**
First, make a brine by dissolving the sea salt in 4 litres of water in a large pan over a low heat. Once the salt has dissolved, remove the pan from the heat and let the brine cool.

Cut a tiny slit in the side of each olive. Be careful not to cut the pits, which if damaged will release a bitter chemical that will ruin the entire job. Tip the prepared olives into a sterilized glass jar (or two) and cover with the brine solution. Store the jar(s) in a cool, dark place (or at the back of the fridge if your house gets too hot) and turn over the olives once a day.

After a few weeks, begin taste-testing your olives until they have reached the desired stage of curing (leave them longer if you want sweeter olives or remove them earlier if you like them bitter as I do).

When you're happy, drain the olives, discarding any that have spoiled, then rinse with fresh water and leave to dry. Wash and sterilize the jars with boiling water and then leave them to dry. Fill the jars with the olives and top with olive oil and your choice of flavourings (lemon peel, bay leaves, rosemary, chilli peppers, garlic cloves, peppercorns or whatever you like). Enjoy the olives and the oil for amazing flavoured dressing on green leaf salads or baked potatoes.

My Middle East experience is thin, but brief stints in Jordan and Israel are enough for me to know that in the Arab world of pulses, chickpeas are king. The chef in me immediately thinks of hummus, but preparing and defining that dish is a culinary tradition in which I have no place.

Instead I'm going to remember the first time I really enjoyed chickpeas as more than a smooth onomatopoeic hummus. During my student days, I fed my brain with salty snacks and while the rest of the house slept, I quietly drained tins of chickpeas before coating them in oil, salt, herbs and spices and roasting them until golden and crunchy. Still popping with heat, I returned to my studies, and while monetary and fiscal policy may have remained confusingly simplistic, the chickpeas made complete complex sense.

# ROASTED
# CHICKPEAS
## WITH ROSEMARY AND LEMON

**60 MIN**

**Ingredients**

200g dried chickpeas or 360g tinned chickpeas, drained

3 bay leaves

4 tbsp finely chopped rosemary leaves

Zest of 1 lemon

Extra-virgin olive oil

Salt and cracked black pepper

**Method**

If you're using dried chickpeas, soak them in water overnight, then drain and rinse them. Cook in boiling water along with a few bay leaves for about 40 minutes until al dente, then drain and set aside to cool.

Preheat the oven to 180°C/Gas Mark 4. Combine the chickpeas with the rosemary, lemon zest, olive oil, a pinch of salt and cracked black pepper and toss to coat. Spread the mixture on a baking tray, then transfer to the oven and roast for 15 minutes until chickpeas are beginning to turn golden. Shake the tray and return the chickpeas to the oven for a further 5 minutes. Serve hot.

If you are lucky enough to get to know Arabic culture, even briefly, you'll know that the only drink to serve with these salty snacks is arak.

Not all anchovies are created equal. They fill the oceans for a higher purpose than to be stretched over tired pizzas and baked until dry and grey or thrown over the side of the boat as part of the 'chum bucket'. The anchovy is an ingredient for the purist: clean and sharp, anchovies are the ocean's salt and the Parmesan of the sea, giving flavour and interest to even the blandest base. Anchovies should be meaty and luscious with a creamy brininess that gives way to a savoury sweetness.

From northern Cantabria to Catalonia's L'Escala, Spain has some of the best. Hands down, the Ortiz brand is king. The anchovy is the closest you will get to taking in big gulps of the Mediterranean, and I eat them naked (the anchovies, not me) and can't think of a recipe that does them justice, so prefer to use *boquerones* (white anchovies) when preparing creative *banderillas*.

# THE BANDERILLA

**15 MIN**

### Ingredients
10 boquerones
20 Sevillana olives (sweet green olives)
10 cherry tomatoes

### Method
The *banderilla* can be as extravagant as the occasion calls for, but use the following flavour combination as your base. Wrap the boquerones around half the olives and spear with a tooth pick together with a cherry tomato and a plain olive. Serve with a chilled glass of local vermouth and you might begin to understand why the Spanish have life sorted.

Is there anything more romantic than skipping through a dense forest, basket in hand, with eyes peeled for the bright yellow, white or golden flash of wild mushrooms? In Catalonia, no fungus is as prized as the *rovelló*, collected in autumn and affectionately named 'Golden Fungus of the Gods'. With poisoned sitting next to prized, wild mushrooms are there only for the brave. For the rest of the world, the basic button can also be something truly glorious.

It was at my grandparent's beach house in Torredembarra, where a pinecone-laden tree shaded the garden, where I discovered the buttery flavour of the pine nut. After painstakingly extracting a handful of the kernels, I found a mortar and pestle to pound them with garlic, Manchego, oil, sherry vinegar, thyme and salt into a creamy white pesto – the perfect filling for the button mushroom. Save the forests for getting hopelessly romantically lost and focus on bringing those brown button-filled supermarket bags to life.

# GRILLED MUSHROOMS
## WITH WHITE PESTO

**20 MIN**

### Ingredients

75g pine nuts, plus extra to serve
2 garlic cloves
100g Manchego cheese, grated, plus extra to serve
1 tsp thyme leaves, plus extra to serve
2 tbsp sherry vinegar

Zest of 1 lemon
Extra-virgin olive oil
500g mushrooms, stalks removed
Salt

### Method

Toast the pine nuts under a hot grill for 5 minutes until golden, then remove and transfer to a food processor. Add the garlic, Manchego, thyme leaves, sherry vinegar, lemon zest, olive oil and a pinch of salt and blend until smooth. Taste and adjust seasoning, if necessary – adding sherry vinegar for more bite or Manchego and oil for a smoother flavour – then set aside.

Place the mushrooms on a baking tray, stalk sides up. Cook under a hot grill for 5 minutes, then remove them and fill each mushroom with spoonfuls of pesto. Return the filled mushrooms to the grill for a further 10 minutes, until the pesto is beginning to bubble and turn golden.

Serve the filled mushrooms with additional pine nuts and some thyme leaves sprinkled over the top, and a drizzle of oil.

**61**

You find meatballs (*albondigas*) in tapas bars throughout Spain – served in miniature *cazuela* dishes with toothpicks, they are the ultimate winter snack. The Australian version didn't inspire – small and salty and generally heaped through pots of spaghetti until the sum of its parts became a meal. My next experience was on a flight to Sweden, where two large pink meatballs were served up in a swamp of cream alongside a thick mound of grey mashed potatoes and a fluorescent red jam (the food got a lot better on touchdown). And then in New York I found myself in Lower East Side with a small plate of pappardelle topped with just one massive Italian meatball covered in a blood-red marinara. I knew this Mediterranean-inspired New York version was closer to where my heart wanted to eat, and so when I found myself in Spain, the *albondiga* made sense and all previous meatball sins were forgotten.

# SPANISH MEATBALLS
## WITH ROMESCO

**20 MIN**

### Ingredients

400g pork mince

2 garlic cloves, minced

1 egg, beaten

75g pine nuts, toasted

2 tbsp chopped flat-leaf parsley leaves

1 tbsp sweet paprika

1 tsp cinnamon

2 tsbp extra-virgin olive oil

8 tbsp romesco (see page 21)

50g Manchego cheese

Purple rosemary flowers, to serve

Salt and cracked black pepper

### Method

Using your hands to mix, combine the mince, garlic, egg, pine nuts, parsley, paprika and cinnamon in a large bowl, then season with salt and pepper and mix again. Lightly flour your hands and take a small quantity of the mince mixture to roll into a ball about the size of a large walnut. Repeat until you have used all the mixture, then sprinkle the meatballs with a little more salt. Heat the olive oil in a large frying pan over a high heat until sizzling, then add the meatballs and fry until golden brown. Then turn the heat down and continue to fry until cooked through.

Serve the meatballs in a little bowl and top with romesco, Manchego shavings and rosemary flowers. Avoid the temptation to toss them in a pot of spaghetti – let them own the dish.

In the Mediterranean, celebrations often permit more than a day off work. In Spain, in April, boys and girls of all ages exchange flowers for books to celebrate Sant Jordi. In June, Sant Joan made it acceptable to fling fireworks around the city. But it is the celebration of the humble onion, the Catalan *calçot*, which remains one of my favourites. During the Calçotada season, a series of large fires are lit throughout Catalonia, on which the freshly dug onions are heaped and grilled, after which, in one flowing motion, they are skinned and dipped in *salbitxada* (a fiery sauce similar to romesco). It gets messy and the more wine you drink (using the Catalan *porron*) the less you tend to worry about the blots of red that will invariably end up on your shirt.

By the late afternoon, when cuts of meats and freshly dug vegetables hidden amongst the coals reach a charry, sweet climax, the anticipation and alcohol-induced hunger is palpable. It's definitely not an occasion for that pressed white shirt or first date, as you peel, dip and suck your way to onion heaven. One of the most delicious celebrations and an occasion my sister dubbed the 'magic onion', the Calçotada season serves as a welcome antidote to Spanish winter (mild as it is).

# CALÇOTS
## WITH SALBITXADA

**35 MIN**

### Ingredients
225g calçots – lots of them (thick spring onions or baby leeks are a poor but acceptable substitute)
Romesco (see page 21, but add a pinch of dried chilli flakes)

### Method
Prepare the calçots by cleaning them and trimming the tops. Line a grill pan with foil, then place the grill rack on top. Heat the grill to high. Lay the calçots out on the rack, grill for 10–15 minutes until beginning to blacken, then turn and grill on the other side for another 10 minutes. Once blackened on both sides, remove the calçots from the grill and lay them on sheets of newspaper. Top with another layer of newspaper and carefully roll up into a tight package and set aside for 10 minutes.

To eat, peel the blackened skin off each calçot and drag it through the romesco, then throw your head back, close your eyes and celebrate.

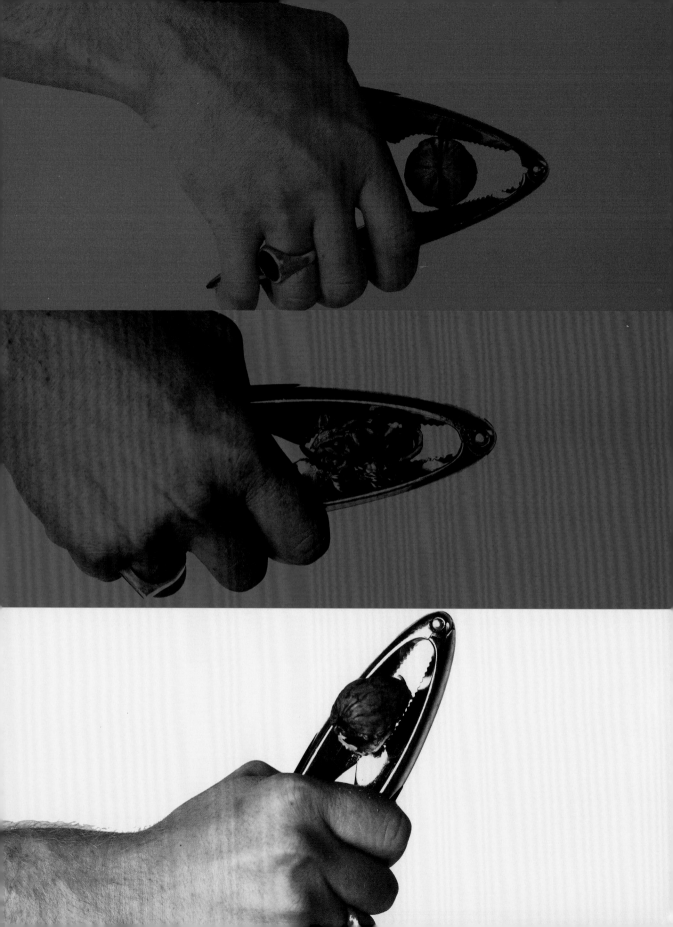

Piquillo peppers, deriving from the Spanish for 'little beak', are another classic tapas, but it wasn't in a bar that I discovered them. Road trips are best when planning is kept to a minimum. So as we hurtled through Catalonia towards the French border, the packet of peanuts began to run low, and we decided next time the road offered up a nice view we would stop for a picnic. This meant the next gas station would serve as the provider of our feast. Prowling the aisles, I found Manchego cheese, a miniature box of green leaves, cubes of quince paste, a yellow plastic tub of allioli and little tins of tuna *escabeche*. What transpired in the next 10 minutes shocked even me: Manchego topped with slivers of quince paste, green leaves with *escabeche* vinegar, and plump smoky piquillo peppers filled with tuna allioli. Eaten on a random concrete bench looking towards the postcard-like snow-capped Alps, I learnt that the best picnics are always spontaneous and that taste is a volatile variable, influenced wildly by where and with whom you are sharing the spread.

# PIQUILLO PEPPERS
## FILLED WITH ORANGE GOATS' CHEESE
## AND WALNUT CRUMBLE

**20 MIN**

### Ingredients

100g soft goats' cheese

Zest and juice of 1 orange

100g finely chopped toasted walnuts

2 tbsp sherry vinegar

1 tsp rosemary, chopped finely

2 tsp chopped thyme leaves, plus extra for sprinkling

8 piquillo peppers (fresh or jarred are equally good), slit open

Extra-virgin olive oil

Salt and cracked black pepper

### Method

Use a fork to combine the goats' cheese with the orange zest and juice, 90g of the chopped walnuts, sherry vinegar, rosemary, thyme and a pinch of salt, until smooth. Carefully open up each pepper and fill it with the goats' cheese mixture. Arrange the filled peppers on a plate and top with a drizzle of olive oil and cracked black pepper. Crumble and sprinkle over some leftover walnuts and thyme leaves. In the summer, chill the filled peppers and serve with crackers; in the winter, place the filled peppers under a medium-hot grill for 10 minutes and serve with a crusty baguette to mop up the delicious melted juice.

Despite settling some 20,000 kilometres from her Spanish heritage, my mother managed to retain the integrity of one dish that remains the domain of all Spanish mothers. It's not sexist – it just is. The tortilla I grew up with was made in a weighty, chipped, black cast-iron pan – the ownership of which my siblings and I still fight.

Tortilla appeared on Mondays – a long day of school that led into an afternoon of tennis practice and an evening of orchestra rehearsal (I was raised by a Tiger-mother). But it was all worth the pain when I barged through the door to the sweet smoky aroma of caramelized onions, fresh purple thyme and fried potatoes. The golden tortilla is a meal all on its own and the inevitable leftovers guaranteed for sandwiches the following day at school. Little did my playground companions know, with their white-bread sandwiches filled with cartoon-like pink meat and plastic cheese, that my tortilla sandwich – jeered at by the unwitting brats – was the same one revered in tapas bars across Spain.

This was no limp omelette or papery crêpe, but a wedge of strength that inspired bravery and spirit. There is a reason the tortilla remains Spain's national tapa and one I continue to rely on as fuel for endless adventures. Long live my mother, Spain and the tortilla.

# THE SPANISH
# TORTILLA

**40** MIN

## Ingredients

2 starchy potatoes (such as russet or Idaho), cut into little cubes
Extra-virgin olive oil
3 thyme sprigs, leaves picked, plus extra for sprinkling
2 onions, halved and thinly sliced
8 eggs
Salt and cracked black pepper

## Method

Experiment with these basic steps and develop something worth handing down to your own children. Soak the potato cubes in water for 5 minutes to remove excess starch, then drain and set aside to dry. Heat the olive oil in a heavy-based frying pan and, once hot, add the potatoes with a pinch of salt and thyme leaves. Fry the potatoes until golden, then reduce the heat and cook for a further 5 minutes until tender. Remove the potato from the pan with a slotted spoon. Add another glug of oil to the pan and tip in the diced onion. Fry on a low heat for 15 minutes until translucent, then remove and set aside.

In a bowl, beat the eggs with a pinch of salt until frothy, then add the potatoes and onions and combine. Heat some more oil in the original pan and, once hot, pour in the tortilla mixture and fry over low heat for 5 minutes, until the eggs have begun to set. Lower the heat and cook for another 5 minutes. To flip the tortilla, place a plate over the pan and in a flowing motion flip the pan upside down so that the tortilla tips out onto the plate. Then, slide the tortilla back into the pan. Fry for a further 2 minutes, until a crust has formed on the underside but the centre remains slightly gooey, then remove from the heat.

Transfer the finished tortilla to a serving plate and top with fresh thyme leaves and a pinch of salt, then cut into wedges and serve. It is best served fresh, but almost as good the next day stuffed between bread with lashings of allioli.

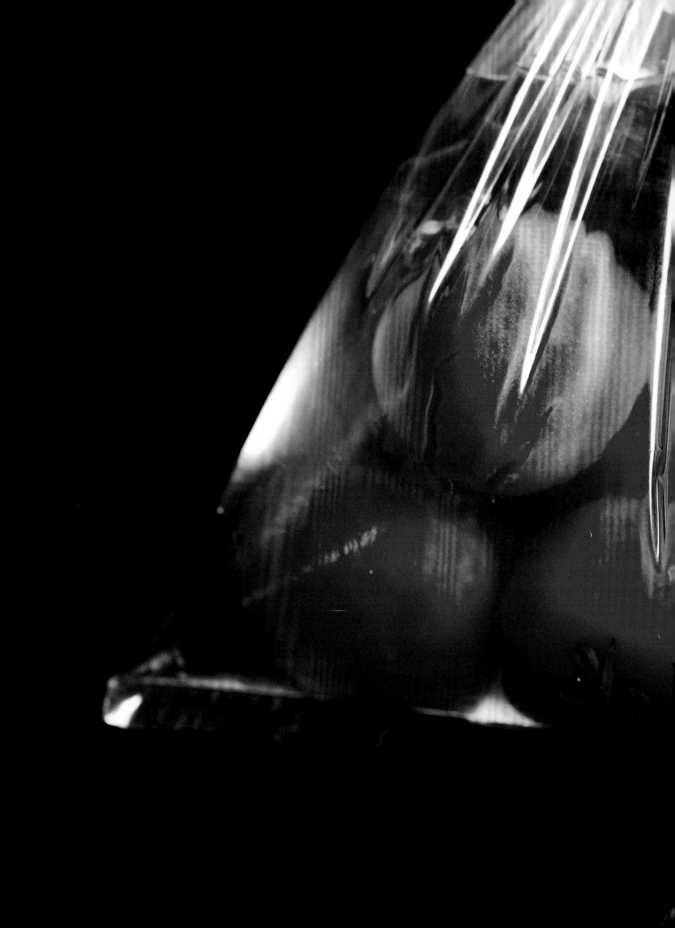

# SOUPS

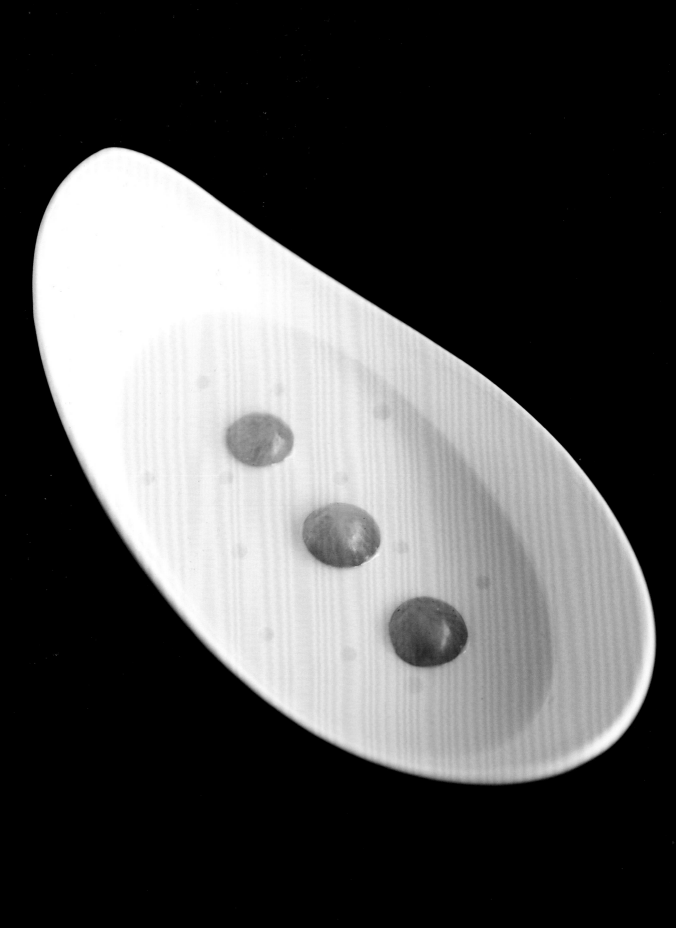

If I had to choose a last meal on death row, I would select *ajo blanco* without hesitation – the silky white colour with the smooth cream of almonds, punch of garlic, kick of sherry vinegar and gloss of olive oil. With any luck, the way I would go wouldn't be by injection or chair, but by drowning in the stuff.

I never tasted the crude *ajo blanco* Papa Serra made (garlic soup and five-year-old don't mix well), so it wasn't until I went on holiday to southern Spain in my early and gastronomically formative twenties that I understood how one could find happiness in a bowl of almonds, garlic, oil and vinegar. The Andalusian version is milky white from the almonds and served with giant green grapes, providing a sweet pop on every spoon. As I sat there looking out towards the Sierra Nevada I knew that when it all ends, it will be a bowl of *ajo blanco* that I hope will pass my lips and, with garlic on my breath, rule out any chance of a farewell kiss.

# AJO BLANCO
## WITH GREEN GRAPES

**30 MIN**

## Ingredients
140g almonds
2 garlic cloves
A chunk of bread, soaked in water
5 tbsp sherry vinegar
Juice of ½ lemon
180ml extra-virgin olive oil, plus extra for drizzling
Salt
100g green grapes, halved and deseeded

## Method
Blanch the almonds in boiling water for 2 minutes, then refresh in cold water and squeeze off the skins. Using a mortar and pestle, grind the garlic with a pinch of salt, then scoop the paste into a blender and add the pre-soaked bread along with its water and the sherry vinegar, lemon juice, olive oil and almonds. Season with salt, then blend for several minutes until completely smooth, adding more of any ingredient until the taste and texture is to your liking. Set the mixture aside to chill in the fridge. To serve, pour the soup into a bowl, then top with a few grapes and a drizzle of olive oil.

Long before the world went mad for longevity and service stations filled drinks cabinets with smoothies of kale and spirulina, I used to hide my morning routine of magic green powders. While putting my body through hell training for a triathlon, partially destroying my kidneys, and more than once finding myself in hospital due to overtraining, I started to furiously teach myself everything there is to know about food as thy medicine (hat tip to Socrates). Once back on my feet, I put my study into practice. After the obligatory swim/bike/run start to the day, I would heap anything with a green hue into the blender – cucumber, lettuce, spinach, mint, celery, seaweed, green peppers, and, of course, today's green lovechild: kale. It was so bad it had to be good for you. I alternated with fruit, nuts and honey and finally found a blend that looked and tasted slightly better than the sludge consumed in *The Matrix*, or today's *Soylent*.

Living in Spain has softened me and mornings are more about some light breaststroke in the Mediterranean, coffee and sunny terraces than they are about laps in chlorinated pools and jugs of green power before the sun has had a chance to rise. But I still blend. Green gazpacho pays homage to a dark past and can bask proudly in the Iberian sun. It's something you can enjoy in sunglasses and with a silver spoon instead of being urgently chugged while still dripping in sweat.

## 20 MIN

# GREEN **GAZPACHO**

### Ingredients

A handful of basil leaves

1 tbsp chopped fresh parsley

½ garlic clove

1 tbsp capers

2 green tomatoes (tomatillos if you can find them)

1 green pepper, deseeded and roughly chopped

Juice of 1 lime

¼ red onion, roughly chopped

1 cucumber, peeled and roughly chopped

1 avocado

30g baby spinach leaves

75g blanched almonds

½ green chilli, seeded

A handful of mint leaves

4 tbsp extra-virgin olive oil

2 tbsp sherry vinegar

Salt

To garnish:

125ml plain yogurt

1 tsp sumac

A handful of blueberries

1 tsp pink peppercorns

A pinch of black salt (hard to find, but worth the effort)

### Method

Setting aside the olive oil and sherry vinegar, pack the rest of the ingredients into a blender or food processor and add a little water, then blend until smooth – add more water until you achieve your desired consistency. Then add the olive oil and sherry vinegar and season with salt to taste. Chill for 1–2 hours, then pour into bowls. Mix together the yogurt and sumac to give a pink mixture, then drizzle a little over each bowl of gazpacho. Top with blueberries, pink peppercorns and black salt.

I always questioned whether soups deserved to qualify as a meal. The act of chewing is so fundamentally tied to pleasure that it took me a while to accept this gastronomic world order. In the heat of a Spanish summer, cold soups are king, but at no point should you ever consider the popular gazpacho to be simply glorified tomato juice. With half a garden in a glass, gazpacho is a meal and deserves to be treated as such. Dress it up with hard-boiled quail eggs, cubes of aged Manchego, black olives, toasted nuts and diced pear. Go one step further and top the soup with a dollop of allioli and you will have the pleasure of getting to know gazpachuelo.

# GAZPACHUELO

**15 MIN**

## Ingredients

4 ripe tomatoes

1 red pepper, roughly chopped

¼ red onion, roughly chopped

½ cucumber, roughly chopped

3 slices of bread, soaked in water

2 tbsp sherry vinegar

4 tbsp olive oil

Salt

Allioli (see page 17)

Garnishes:

Olive oil

2 slices of bread, for croutons

5 Spanish black olives, sliced thinly

2 jamón slices, torn

¼ red pepper, chopped

2 ripe tomatoes, chopped

200g queso fresco, chopped into small cubes

## Method

Blanch the tomatoes in boiling water for 30 seconds, then remove with a slotted spoon and transfer to a bowl of iced water. Peel off the skins. Place the skinned tomatoes in a blender or food processor along with the red pepper, red onion, cucumber, bread and its soaking water, sherry vinegar and olive oil. Season with salt. Blend for 3 minutes until smooth, then taste and adjust the seasoning, if necessary. Strain the mixture through a sieve and transfer to the fridge to chill.

For the garnish, heat a glug of oil in a pan, then add the cubes of bread and gently fry until golden, then set aside. Prepare the other garnishes into separate serving bowls. Spread the allioli around the edges of the bowls, then ladle in chilled gazpacho. Serve the garnishes alongside.

Having only ever visited Spain for summer holidays (basically, any one of the 200 days the country enjoys sunshine), I eagerly anticipated my first winter living in Barcelona. Not for the empty streets following the exodus of jamón-munching summer tourists, but also for the excuse to actually sit down inside a restaurant. Indoor sit-down meals, when the heat still hangs in the sky and sun-drenched squares remain filled with life, are to be avoided at all costs. So it took a particularly chilly December evening to entice me to visit a cave-like restaurant that seemed to source its heating and aroma from ovens loaded with legs of lamb and overflowing pots of shellfish – environmentally and gastronomically aligned to all my beliefs. Fate drew my eyes to the scrawled menu where I spotted the magical-sounding *suquet de peix* (a Catalan fish stew). My dining partner and I found a table. Two large *cazuelas* were promptly plonked down in front of us. Our eyes widened to match the size of the briny clam shells poking out among a savoury *umami* (broth) thick with hunks of monkfish and bright orange mussels. Winter is short and sharp in Barcelona, but *suquet* makes it a worthwhile season in its own right.

# ROMESCO DE PEIX
# (ROMESCO FISH SOUP)

**60** MIN

## Ingredients

500g mussels

500g clams

500g monkfish (or other firm white fish fillet), skin removed and cut into chunks

1 egg yolk, beaten

50g plain flour

4 tbsp extra-virgin olive oil, plus extra to serve

235ml dry white wine

3 bay leaves

A pinch of saffron

2 potatoes, peeled and cut into small wedges

2 onions, chopped

3 garlic cloves, diced

1 ñora pepper, rehydrated in water (ancho chilli or another smoky version is fine)

2 tsp sweet smoked paprika

750ml seafood fumet (see page 27)

6 slices crusty bread, toasted

3 tbsp romesco, plus extra to serve (see page 21)

A handful of fresh parsley, finely chopped

Salt and cracked black pepper

## Method

Prepare mussels and clams by scrubbing them under running water and removing their beards and any grit, then set aside. Dredge the chunks of fish through the beaten egg yolk, then coat in the flour. Heat oil in a large saucepan over a high heat and fry the fish until golden on both sides, then remove the fish using a slotted spoon and set aside. Pour the white wine into the same pan along with a bay leaf, then add the mussels and clams and cover with a lid. Cook over a medium heat until the shells are halfway open, then remove the shellfish (discarding any that haven't opened) using a slotted spoon and set aside. Strain the liquid into a bowl and add the saffron threads.

Heat the remaining oil in a large pot and sauté the chunks of potato and the onion, garlic, ñora pepper and remaining bay leaves until the onion is translucent. Add the sweet smoked paprika and leave to fry for another 5 minutes. Add the wine and bring to a simmer, then add the seafood fumet and simmer for a further 5 minutes. Add the fish, seafood and romesco, turn down the heat to low and leave to simmer until ready to serve.

Ladle the soup into bowls and serve with a wedge of bread slathered with romesco. Drizzle with olive oil, garnish with the parsley and a pinch of sweet smoked paprika, then huddle up to someone you love and dig in.

# VEGETABLES

Heading into London's bleak January, I knew an escape to the Mediterranean (where winter is more a concept than a season) was obligatory for my survival. Madrid was calling and, making sure not to reveal my Barça loyalties, I dedicated the week to eating everything and anything. This culinary embrace of a city that is already intoxicating for the gastronome found me on a diet of sandwiches filled with crunchy, golden calamari for breakfast, *cocido* and *callos* for lunch, and *churros* with black Spanish chocolate in the evening. And that's not even counting the jamón and queso that graced the start of every meal.

Needless to say, I returned to London yearning for a detox. Something fresh, something clean; hell, a bite out of a vegan would have satisfied my green lust. I threw together a green salad on arrival, and stuffed myself with leaves until I felt like I could manage a walk in the park without gazing longingly at fresh-cut grass. Spain taught me to forget about tomorrow, or the next day, and enjoy the present in all its sinful deliciousness.

# BECAUSE ACTUALLY SOME GREAT STORIES STARTED WITH SOMEONE EATING A SALAD

### Ingredients

3 dried bay leaves

35g pine nuts

1 garlic clove, diced

2 tbsp capers

2 tbsp flat-leaf parsley leaves

Juice of 1 lemon

50ml extra-virgin olive oil, plus extra for frying

1 head of green chicory

1 head of butter lettuce

100g rocket

100g baby spinach

200g mangetout

Zest and juice of 1 lime

3 tbsp sherry vinegar

200g queso fresco

4 tbsp torn basil leaves

Seeds of 1 pomegranate

Salt and cracked black pepper

# GREEN SALAD

**15 MIN**

## Method

Preheat the oven to 130°C/Gas Mark ½. Using a mortar and pestle, grind the dried bay leaves with a pinch of salt to a powder, then set aside. Spread the pine nuts on a tray and roast in the oven for 5 minutes, until golden, then remove and let cool for a few minutes. Using a mortar and pestle, grind the pine nuts with the garlic, capers, parsley, basil, lemon juice and 3 tablespoons of the olive oil to a pesto, season to taste, then set aside.

Separate the leaves from the heads of green chicory and butter lettuce, then wash them and shake dry. Roughly chop, mix them with the rocket and baby spinach leaves and set aside. Heat a lug of oil in a small pan over a medium heat. Add the mangetout to the pan with a pinch of salt. Once the mangetout have begun to soften, remove from the heat and set aside.

In the base of a salad bowl, mix the remaining olive oil, lime juice and sherry vinegar. Add the green leaves and the fresh and fried mangetout and toss lightly.

Serve the salad on a large plate and decorate with spoons of the pesto, chunks of queso fresco, torn basil leaves and pomegranate seeds, then dust with the ground bay leaf powder.

It wasn't until I went to the Levant – that rich part of the world with a food culture that rivals the Mediterranean – that I understood the full potential of the aubergine with its blackened skin and savoury flesh.

In Spain its popularity comes in the form of *escalivada*, a delicious cliché that pairs grilled aubergine with peppers and courgettes. The aubergine is more popular in the south of Spain, where the Moors introduced it with mint, cumin, sumac and honey. Although Spain has adopted the exotic fruit, it has yet to fully embrace its potential. Despite only making it to the Levant at most once a year, I give headaches to every border guard who must carefully open, sniff and approve each of my vacuum-packed bags of spices. In my small kitchen back home, I coat the grilled aubergine in sumac, roast it with za'atar and season fried hunks of it with honey and *dukkah* – paying homage to the very special Levant.

# ROASTED AUBERGINES
## WITH FRESH CHEESE AND GREEN OLIVE PESTO

**40** MIN

## Ingredients

2 aubergines, cut in half lengthways

50ml extra-virgin olive oil

1 onion

2 garlic cloves, chopped

1 bay leaf

4 tomatoes, chopped

1 green pepper, seeded and chopped

40g raisins, soaked in water and finely chopped

2 tbsp chopped mint leaves

Zest and juice of 1 lemon

1 tbsp fennel seeds, ground

1 tbsp sweet paprika

1 tsp cinnamon

70g almonds, toasted

75g green olives, stoned and chopped

2 tbsp chopped flat-leaf parsley leaves

3 tbsp sherry vinegar

200g queso fresco, thinly sliced

50g walnuts, toasted and roughly chopped

A pinch of smoked paprika

Salt and cracked black pepper

## Method

Heat the grill to medium-hot. Lay the aubergine halves cut-side up on a baking tray. Score the flesh, then drizzle with 2 tablespoons of the oil and rub a little salt into the cuts. Place under the grill for 15 minutes, until the flesh is soft. Scoop most of the flesh out into a bowl and set the skins aside. Heat some more oil in a saucepan, then add the onion, 1 garlic clove, the bay leaf and a pinch of salt and fry for 5 minutes until beginning to soften. Add the tomatoes and green pepper and fry until the tomatoes have broken down. Next, add the aubergine flesh, raisins, mint, most of the lemon zest and juice, the ground fennel seeds, sweet paprika and cinnamon and leave for another 10 minutes until thickened.

To make the pesto topping, put the almonds, 1 garlic clove, olives, most of the parsley, and sherry vinegar in a blender or food processor. Add a drizzle of olive oil and season with a pinch of salt and cracked black pepper and blend to a pesto-like consistency, then set aside. Place the aubergine skins on a baking tray and fill with the aubergine-flesh mixture and top with thin slices of cheese. Grill until cheese is beginning to melt, then remove from the grill and transfer to a serving plate. Top each half with the pesto, walnuts, a pinch of smoked paprika, and the remainder of the parsley and lemon zest and juice.

# VEGETARIANS:
## TAPAS DO ACTUALLY EXTEND
# BEYOND THE POTATO

Going through heartbreak affects people differently. My coping mechanism has been to spend more hours running through black Melbourne nights, substituting sleep for hours spent writing recipes and sating my drunk appetite with the healthy man's snack of carrots dipped in peanut butter. With this beta-carotene overload, my skin turned an orange tinge that my mother first noticed during her visits once every few months. She rightly exclaimed: 'You're turning into a carrot!' Others were equally subtle, asking me what brand of fake tan I was using.

Carrots thus formed the basis of my signature dish that was simple and fresh. I first discovered it in Morocco, where ceramic bowls were filled with chunks of carrots basting in a pungent combination of fresh mint, orange juice and toasted cumin, served alongside hot glasses of the ubiquitous mint tea to complete the exotic picture. I returned to Barcelona still licking my lips, and set about stamping Spain all over it.

# SPICED CARROTS 25 MIN

## Ingredients

4 carrots
Zest and juice of 1 orange
2 tbsp sherry vinegar
1 tsp cumin
260g salsa verde (see page 23)
50g almonds, toasted
1 tbsp sumac
A handful of mint leaves
60g plain yogurt
Seeds of 1 pomegranate

## Method

Fill a large saucepan with cold water, then add the whole trimmed carrots, place over a high heat and bring to the boil. Reduce the heat to medium-low and simmer the carrots until al dente. Drain, then peel while still hot, slice into small rounds and set aside. In a separate bowl, combine the orange juice, sherry vinegar and cumin to make a marinade. Tip the marinade and the salsa verde into the bowl with the carrots and stir through to coat. Place the almonds and the sumac into a blender and whizz to a rough crunch. Using a hand-held blender, whizz the mint leaves with a little yogurt to create a purée, then fold in the remainder of the yogurt. To serve, drizzle a little of the mint yogurt on a plate then top with a scoop of carrots and dress with sumac almond crunch and pomegranate seeds.

A zesty side-dish or stand-alone tapa – this dish is enough to maintain that orange beta-carotene glow for all the right reasons.

In my local mercat de Santa Caterina exists tomato paradise (enter, turn left and walk to the end – I'm not sharing any more details). Last count there were sixteen varietals on sale, not counting the ones Jordi keeps behind the counter for foodie types like myself. They range from the exotic tiger-striped, the sweet yellow cherry and the sensuous Montserrat to the almost pornographic Barbastro – crimson red and splitting with sweet red juice – and my favourite, the crisp sour-green variety that need little more than oil and salt to be properly savoured.

I have lived through the depths of London winter and the glorious peak of Barcelona summer, and if there is one ingredient that captured my mood across the two scenarios, it is the tomato. The British supermarket offers a solid orange sphere of watery misery, while Barcelona offers glorious red hues of sweet juicy fruit that fill more than your mouth with pure Mediterranean pleasure.

# TOMATOES

**150 MIN**

## Ingredients

5 tbsp torn basil leaves

50ml extra-virgin olive oil

1 tbsp balsamic vinegar

1 tsp caster sugar

8 Roma (plum) tomatoes

1 tbsp of thyme leaves

4 heirloom tomatoes

5 baby artichokes, cooked and peeled (or buy prepared ones from the delicatessen)

35g blanched almonds

50g black olives

Zest and juice of 1 lime

10 cherry tomatoes, halved

1 ball fresh burrata

35g pine nuts, toasted

50g of Manchego cheese

Salt and cracked black pepper

## Method

Preheat the oven to 80°C/Gas Mark ¼. Using a mortar and pestle, grind the basil leaves (reserve a few for presentation) with salt and a lug of oil until shiny, then set aside. In a small saucepan, simmer the balsamic vinegar with the sugar until syrupy, then set aside.

Cut off the tops of the Roma tomatoes and scoop out the seeds, taking care to preserve the tomatoes' cylindrical form. Set aside the seeds on a plate and place the deseeded shells on a baking tray. Sprinkle with thyme and season with cracked black pepper and salt. Place the baking tray in the oven for about 2 hours, then remove and set aside.

Finely slice the heirloom tomatoes into thin rounds and set aside. Make a tapenade by blending the olives and almonds in a food processor with the lime zest and juice, a drizzle of olive oil and a pinch of salt until completely smooth, then set aside.

At this stage you can get creative. Smear the olive tapenade across a plate, arrange the different tomato preparations on top, break open burrata, drizzle over the basil oil, sprinkle over the pine nuts, dot with the balsamic syrup, top with reserved torn basil and shavings of Manchego – food is art so close your eyes and become Dalí just for a moment.

Growing up in Tasmania in Australia, roasted vegetables served as the welcome antidote to cold, windy nights that shook our single-panel wooden house. In sunny Barcelona, roasting is an activity no chef will look forward to outside of those few days the temperature falls into single digits. An evening meal of heaving hot plates of food seems so foreign now; instead I usually find myself at tables filled with pickled and cured bites that demand little more than toothpicks as utensils. But I sometimes miss the deep, wholesome satisfaction of the roast. In Tasmania, root vegetables were muddled with thick bunches of rosemary and thyme and strips of zesty lemon, then doused in rock salt and olive oil before being roasted, then emerging from the oven, golden and glorious. Save roasting for that grey day when the chill is real and your fingers are too cold to properly clasp toothpicks. On that day, this is your recipe.

# STICKY MEMBRILLO
# PUMPKIN
## WITH ALMOND CREAM
## AND CRISPY PURPLE RADICCHIO

**30 MIN**

## Ingredients

70g almonds, blanched and deskinned

3 tbsp sherry vinegar

40ml extra-virgin olive oil

1 small butternut squash, peeled, deseeded and sliced into thick rounds

2 tbsp thyme leaves

100g membrillo (quince paste)

1 tbsp nigella seeds

2 tsp edible thyme flowers

Salt and cracked black pepper

## Method

Preheat the oven to 180°C/Gas Mark 4. Put the almonds, sherry vinegar and 30ml of the olive oil in a blender. Season with salt and blend until smooth, then set aside. Toss the rounds of butternut squash with the remaining olive oil and thyme leaves. Season with cracked black pepper and pinch of salt and mix again. Transfer to a baking tray and top with a thin slice of membrillo. Place in the oven and roast for 20 minutes until the squash is sticky and soft.

Put the almond cream in a bowl, then top with the roasted squash and finish with nigella seeds and the thyme flowers. And if you are that way inclined, throw a bird in the oven with more vegetables, halved lemons, copious cloves of garlic and fat handfuls of herbs such as rosemary, thyme and bay. Winter will never be something to fear again.

There aren't many sauces in the world that inspire a route of their own, but *xató* is one of them. The Ruta del Xató is a trek that begins in the Spanish seaside town of Sitges, snakes inwards to Vilafranca del Penedès, then on to El Vendrell, finally returning again to the sea at Vilanova i la Geltrú.

In Stiges I tasted *xató*, not with the traditional curly endive and anchovies, but over fried eggs with sour green tomatoes for breakfast. It has the nutty richness of romesco, but with the salty kick of anchovy and fresh green of parsley. It was deep and authentic and the perfect foil to the flashy brash glow the city takes on in the summer as hoardes of tourists descend upon it. Luckily they order from the English menu filled with bacon, sausages and hash browns, leaving the local secrets to those who arrive not on budget airlines, but having followed at least some part of the Ruta del Xató.

# XATÓ WITH ENDIVE, ANCHOVIES AND ALMONDS

**45 MIN**

## Ingredients

40g raisins

75g cherry tomatoes, halved

2 parsley stalks, chopped

Juice and zest of ½ lemon

5 ñora chillies

35g unblanched almonds, toasted

40g hazelnuts, toasted

1 garlic clove

5 anchovies

300ml sherry vinegar

20ml extra-virgin olive oil

4 eggs

1 crusty baguette

1 tbsp sweet paprika

½ head curly endive, torn apart

1 tbsp smoked paprika

## Method

Preheat the oven to 180°C/Gas Mark 4. Hydrate the raisins by soaking them in some sherry vinegar for at least 30 minutes. Meanwhile, toss the cherry tomatoes with half of the parsley and a quarter of the lemon zest and roast for 10 minutes.

To make the *xató*, hydrate the ñoras in a bowl of warm water, then remove them and cut them open and scrape out the seeds. Place the ñoras in a blender with the almonds, hazelnuts, garlic, 3 anchovies, the rest of the parsley, sherry vinegar and oil, until a thick sauce forms. Taste to adjust the seasoning, then transfer the sauce to the fridge.

Half fill a medium saucepan with cold water, then carefully drop in the eggs. Place the pan over a high heat and bring the water to the boil. Once boiling, remove from the heat and cover with a lid. Leave for 5 minutes, then remove the eggs with a slotted spoon and chill in iced water. Peel the eggs and set aside. Cut the baguette into small chunks, then heat a lug of oil in a frying pan and fry for 5 minutes until you have golden and crunchy croutons. Remove the croutons from the pan and toss with salt and sweet paprika, then set aside.

Decorate a serving plate with endive, roasted cherry tomatoes, xató, croutons, sliced egg, 2 anchovies and smoked paprika, then top with a drizzle of lemon juice and a drizzle of oil.

There is a restaurant just outside of Copenhagen that burned the crispy deliciousness of fennel into my brain. No, it wasn't Noma (I wish), it was a no-name bar where we stopped for a drink of good frothy Danish beer before catching the train back to the capital. With beers drawn, we picked out a few plates from their chalkboard menu. There were the frites, little eggs with mayonnaise, and open rye smørrebrød served with cured trout, but the dish that stunned me in its stark simplicity was a plate of fennel, shaved paper-thin and splashed with green olive oil, then seasoned with impossibly tiny wild berries and black flakes of salt. It was a revelation and had such clarity of flavour that to this day it reminds me of Nordic cuisine: the food is clean, clear and perfectly balanced.

Sharp like radish, crunchy like celery and cool like a cucumber, when the heavy white bulbs start showing up in Spanish markets at the end of summer, it signals the seasons are well and truly changing. Shave them carpaccio-thin while there is still some heat in the sky, then as the relative cold sets in, roast them until they reveal their sweet inner core.

# FENNEL
## CRUSTED in THYME, ALMOND and GARROTXA CHEESE
## with CHERRY TOMATO CONFIT

**45 MIN**

### Ingredients

35g unblanched almonds, toasted

4 thyme sprigs, leaves picked

Zest of 1 lime

30ml extra-virgin olive oil, plus extra for drizzling

75g raisins, finely chopped

100g Garrotxa (Catalan goats' cheese) or other semi-hard cheese

300g cherry tomatoes, halved

1 tbsp fennel seeds, ground

2 fennel bulbs, trimmed, bulbs quartered

120ml white wine

½ lemon

Salt and cracked black pepper

### Method

Preheat the oven to 150°C/Gas Mark 2. Using a mortar and pestle, grind the almonds with most of the thyme leaves, the lime zest, 20ml olive oil, raisins and cheese to form a pesto. Season with salt and pepper.

Lay the cherry tomatoes on a baking tray, skin-side down. Sprinkle them with oil and ground fennel seeds and season with salt and cracked black pepper. Roast in the oven for 20 minutes until beginning to caramelize then set aside.

Toss the fennel bulb quarters with 10ml oil and salt. Place a large frying pan over a medium heat and, once hot, add the fennel. Fry until golden on all sides. Add the wine and cook until all the liquid has evaporated, then remove the fennel from the pan.

Spread the almond pesto over the fennel and place on a baking tray, outer side down. Transfer to the oven and roast for 15 minutes, until the almond crust is golden and crunchy. Remove the fennel from the oven and set aside.

Place a spoon of the tomatoes on a plate and top with the fennel bulbs. Grate lemon zest over the top, sprinkle with the remaining thyme leaves, then drizzle with olive oil and season with salt and cracked black pepper.

I rate curiosity as an obligatory character trait, and even more so for a chef. Maybe this is why I have so much respect for mad guys like the entrepreneur Tim Ferriss and his enthusiasm to test the limits of body and mind using himself as the human guinea pig. I've lived the same way with respect to food: for a while going raw (without going vegetarian – sashimi was the order of the day), and for a while eating as a fruitarian (the theory being that if you eat the entire fruit – skin, seeds and core – you extract a complete set of nutrients). I've tried to replicate the diets of the Peruvians, Japanese and Sardinians (high in fish, fresh vegetables and pickles). These experiments had mixed results, but they are all fun to look back on (although not so much at the time, when dinners consisted of raw steaks rubbed with butter or five solitary pears, depending on what phase I was going through).

I've matured and now believe in refined gluttony as the path to dietary equilibrium. But if I had to choose one more dietary experiment to test, it would be the 'Instincto' theory, where you are permitted to eat just one ingredient each meal. Take beetroot: roasted, steamed, fried, glazed, juiced, braised, pickled and shaved raw – you can fill a plate with beetroot without getting purple fatigue.

Actually, forget the theory, combine the purple root with grassy goats' cheese, sweet tart fruits such as plums or kumquats, the rich oiliness of toasted walnuts and strong herbs such as sage and thyme, and the palette-friendly purple flowers of wild rosemary.

# BEETROOT
## PICKLED IN SHERRY VINEGAR WITH PLUMS, GOATS' CHEESE, THYME AND WALNUT
### 75 MIN

### Ingredients

4 beetroots with leaves

50ml extra-virgin olive oil

235ml apple cider vinegar

Zest and juice of 1 lemon

1 tbsp honey

3 rosemary sprigs

White wine

100g walnuts

2 tbsp natural yogurt

3–4 sprigs of basil, leaves picked

Zest of ½ orange

Capers

Sherry vinegar

2 tbsp thyme, leaves picked

Egg yolk

Breadcrumbs

4 purple plums, destoned

100g soft goats' cheese (chevre is ideal)

Salt and cracked black pepper

### Method

Prepare the beetroot by removing the leaves then scrubbing the root clean of any dirt. Wash the leaves thoroughly, then shake dry and set aside. Cut a cross in the top of one of the beetroots and then drizzle with olive oil and season with salt. Place on the baking tray and transfer to the oven on medium heat for 60 minutes, until tender enough to pierce with a fork. Remove from the oven and chop into rough chunks. Slice a second beetroot and slice into thin discs using a mandolin, then arrange the slices on a serving dish. Mix the apple cider vinegar, lemon juice and honey. Pour the mixture over the beetroot and season with salt. Transfer the beetroot to the fridge and leave to marinate for at least 6 hours. Cut a third beetroot into small cubes. Heat oil in a frying pan and add the beetroot cubes with 2 sprigs of rosemary and a pinch of salt and fry over medium heat for 10 minutes, until beetroot begins to soften, then add a lug of white wine and continue to fry until the liquid has reduced and the beetroot is tender, then set aside. Boil the final beetroot in a pot of water for 20 minutes until tender, then remove and peel.

Place the cooked beetroot in a blender along with 50g of the walnuts, yogurt, a handful of basil leaves, orange zest and capers and blend until completely smooth. Pass the mixture through a fine sieve, then set aside.

Heat a lug of oil in a large saucepan and, once hot, add the beetroot leaves along with a pinch of salt and fry for 5 minutes until wilted, then splash with sherry vinegar and fry for another minute. Remove the leaves from the frying pan and dress with a drizzle of olive oil. Spread the remaining 50g of walnuts on a baking tray and toast for 5 minutes under a hot grill. Using a mortar and pestle, crush the walnuts with thyme leaves, half the lemon zest and some salt to create a crumble, then set aside. Pick the 6 largest basil leaves then coat in egg yolk and then breadcrumbs. Fry the leaves in olive oil until crispy, then remove and dry on paper towel. Arrange three different shapes of beetroot, beetroot leaves and plum wedges on a plate, then drizzle with beetroot purée, crumble with goats' cheese, scatter the fried basil leaves, walnut gremolata and the other sprig of fresh rosemary.

Nothing tells you spring is about to give way to the gloating heat of summer than the courgette flower (in Italian, the operatic sounding *fiori di zucca*). Near my apartment in El Borne, there is a neighbourhood garden where courgette flowers scream out to be picked, filled and fried. I spent afternoons weeding and planting chard and cabbage on this urban plot, simply to feel like I deserved a bulging bag of *fiori*. My food isn't generally pretty and I will always do better with a knife than I will with a paintbrush, but even the roughest plating of these edible joys is destined to be fine and elegant.

# COURGETTE FLOWERS FILLED WITH POPPY SEED CREAM AND POMEGRANATE SYRUP

**30 MIN**

### Ingredients

6 basil leaves

Zest and juice of 1 lemon

6 tbsp mató

2 tbsp apple cider vinegar

¾ litre extra-virgin olive oil

4 tbsp runny honey

40g poppy seeds

Seeds of ½ a pomegranate

1 tbsp caster sugar

12 courgette flowers

2 egg yolks, beaten

60g breadcrumbs

Salt and cracked black pepper

### Method

Place 4 basil leaves with the lemon juice, mató, apple cider vinegar, 4 tablespoons of olive oil, honey and poppy seeds in a blender, season and whizz until smooth. Put the pomegranate seeds in a separate bowl. Use a stick blender to blend them, then strain the juice into a small pan and add the sugar. Simmer the juice over a medium heat until thick and syrupy (about 30 minutes). Set aside.

Meanwhile, gently open the courgette flowers and fill with poppy seed cream. One by one, dip the filled flowers first in the beaten egg yolk then in the breadcrumbs and set aside to dry on a paper towel.

Heat 700ml of oil in a large frying pan over a medium heat. Once the oil is sizzling, drop in the flowers and fry for 5 minutes. Then flip and fry for another 3 minutes until golden on both sides. Serve hot, with pomegranate syrup drizzled over the top, cracked pepper and 2 basil leaves.

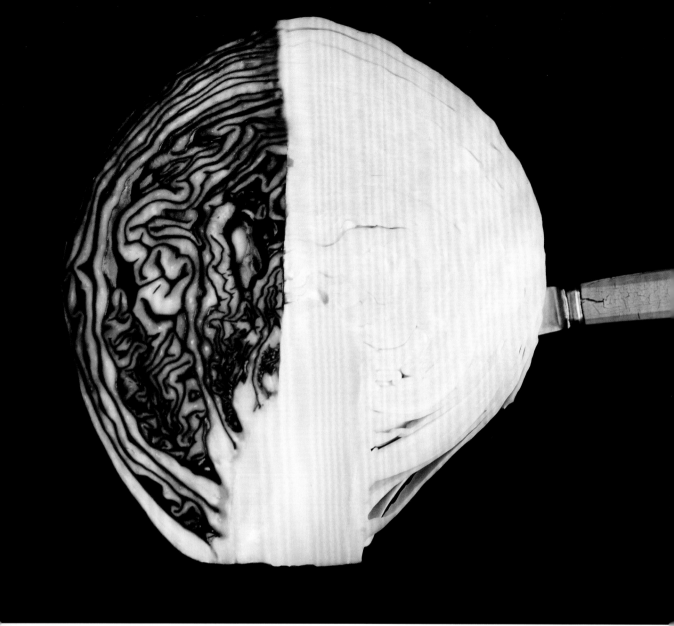

In the world I grew up in, coleslaw is a KFC creation served in small plastic buckets, a fresh trio of cabbage, carrot and onion drowned in an addictive cream of mayonnaise, sugar and vinegar – the perfect acidic foil to a bone of crunchy fried chicken.

Southern Spain is known for its reliance on the deep-fryer, and most of the time it demonstrates a dexterity that shows up in *puntillitas*, *tortilla de camarones*, *chocos*, *ortiguillas*, *chipirones* or *berengenas con miel* (Google the names and add them to your gourmet bucket list). But sometimes a tangy offset is required – even KFC acknowledges this fact. Andalusia would do well to follow the Colonel's lead and introduce coleslaw as the side dish of choice and help gluttons like me extend deep-fried sessions into all-day affairs.

# SPANISH COLESLAW WITH GRAPES AND SEEDS

**30** MIN

## Ingredients

10ml extra-virgin olive oil

3 tbsp apple cider vinegar

1 tsp wholegrain mustard

1 tsp brown sugar

2 tbsp dried oregano

Juice of 1 lemon

¼ head of green cabbage, shredded

¼ head of purple cabbage, shredded

½ red onion, finely sliced

30g black grapes, peeled and quartered

30g green grapes, peeled and quartered

½ green pepper, finely sliced

125g natural Greek yogurt

1 garlic clove, crushed

2 handfuls of parsley, finely chopped

3 tbsp sweet paprika, plus extra for dusting

½ tsp cinnamon

4 tbsp sunflower seeds, toasted

4 tbsp pumpkin seeds, toasted

## Method

In a large bowl, combine the olive oil, apple cider vinegar, mustard, brown sugar, dried oregano and half the lemon juice to form a vinaigrette. Add the cabbage (green and purple), onion, grapes and pepper and fully coat in the dressing. Set aside.

In a separate bowl, mix the yogurt, garlic, parsley, remaining lemon juice, sweet paprika and cinnamon.

Add the yogurt mixture to the cabbage mixture and combine thoroughly. Serve sprinkled with the sunflower and pumpkin seeds and dusted with a little extra sweet paprika. Ideally, serve on a crowded table filled with all manner of crispy, crunchy golden delights and not a white and red plastic tub in sight.

Brassicas aren't regular features on the Spanish table, but the cauliflower deserves more air-time. In Spain, I've found only the white florets pickled and served with olives, silvery anchovies and icy glasses of vermouth. But it doesn't have to be so. The French have long recognized cauliflower's potential, puréeing it and using it as a silky base for caramelized scallops and grilled with Gruyère cheese to create a luscious gratin (think mac 'n' cheese in a tuxedo).

Bold Iberian flavours, such as anchovies, pickled capers and spicy chorizo, are the perfect match for the cauliflower's creamy nuttiness, and there is no reason Spain shouldn't also celebrate one of the most unassuming and underrated vegetables.

# SAFFRON ROASTED
# CAULIFLOWER
## WITH PINE NUTS AND CURRANTS

**30 MIN**

## Ingredients

235ml dry white wine

A small pinch of saffron threads

1 strip lemon peel

1 cauliflower, separated into florets

20ml extra-virgin olive oil

2 shallots, halved and thinly sliced

1 bay leaf

1 garlic clove, chopped

35g currants

2 tbsp capers

2 tsp sherry vinegar

35g pine nuts, toasted and
  chopped

100g dried breadcrumbs

50g Manchego

3 thyme sprigs, leaves picked,
  reserving any flowers to
  decorate

Zest and juice of 1 lemon

Salt and cracked black pepper

## Method

Pour the wine into a cup and add the saffron. Leave to steep for 10 minutes until the colour begins to bleed. Meanwhile, put the lemon juice in a large bowl, add a pinch of salt and the cauliflower and toss to combine. Heat a lug of oil in a large saucepan and fry the shallots with the bay leaf, garlic and seasoning over a medium heat for about 10 minutes, until the shallots are soft and translucent.

Once the shallots are translucent, add the saffron and wine mixture, currants and one strip of lemon peel and bring to a simmer. Add the cauliflower and capers and continue to simmer over a low heat for about 10 minutes, until the liquid has evaporated and the cauliflower is tender. Remove from the heat, splash in the sherry vinegar, then set aside.

Heat the grill to high. Combine the pine nuts, breadcrumbs, Manchego, thyme leaves, salt and lemon zest in a small bowl and season with salt and pepper.

Transfer the cauliflower florets to a baking tray and sprinkle the flavoured crumbs over the top, then drizzle over 10ml olive oil. Place under the grill for 10 minutes, until the crust begins to turn golden.

Serve decorated with purple thyme flowers, if you have any, to contrast the exotic golden colour of saffron.

**105**

# POTATOES

There is a race in Tasmania that sends a few hundred runners hurtling up 20km of mountain (with a gradient of around 9% all the way up) to reach a peak that even in summer is sometimes capped with snow. Training begins a few months beforehand, with time spent not just getting distance into the legs, but also building hard muscle. I treated myself to hill sprints and tortuous stair climbs up Mount Nelson, which together with pool sessions and Pilates, made for a fairly complete routine. Some nights I used to pound up a set of 500 stairs (you get good at counting) a few times a week, and despite almost reaching the point where my body gave me an exhausted and withering glance, I always returned home with a hunger that verged on being dangerous to those nearby.

Arriving home still pulsating with adrenalin, I felt my way around a dark pantry until I grasped the familiar sack of potatoes, every athlete's friend. With spuds in one hand and a large pot in the other, I was well on my way to replacing glycogen stores, and a small part of my soul. I used to boil those potatoes for a few minutes before roughly chopping and dousing them in big lugs of olive oil, freshly chopped rosemary, grated lemon zest, cracked black pepper and rock salt. I then slammed them under the grill for a few minutes, until they began to turn golden and crispy.

With fork in hand, a chipped mug of wine and late-night American talk shows, I proceeded to refuel my body with the most simple of carbohydrates for the mind and body and slowly began to feel human again.

# SALT-BAKED WITH SALSA VERDE

**10** MIN

Baking in salt gives potatoes a nutty richness and leaves them crying out for a fresh zesty salsa like this one that transforms them from spud to stud.

**Ingredients**

4 potatoes, washed (small and waxy – purple if you can find them); 4 tbsp of salsa verde (see page 23); salt

**Method**

Preheat the oven to 180°C/Gas Mark 4. Parboil the potatoes for 5 minutes, then chill under running water and pat dry. Lay the potatoes in a baking dish and sprinkle over 3–4 pinches of salt. Bake in the oven until the skins are beginning to crack, then remove from oven, break open with a fork and top with a dollop of salsa verde

# GRILLED WITH ALLIOLI

**30** MIN

Nothing lifts the humble potato more than a bitey garlicky allioli – baked until a golden crust begins to form.

**Ingredients**

4 potatoes, peeled; 4 tbsp of allioli (see page 17)

**Method**

Preheat the oven to 180°C/Gas Mark 4. Slice the potatoes into 3cm rounds and lay them on a baking tray. Spread them with allioli and transfer to oven. Bake for 30 minutes, until the allioli is golden and the potatoes are tender, then remove from the oven and serve.

# SIMMERED IN SAFFRON

**20** MIN

Golden treasures transformed by the magic flavour and colour of saffron.

**Ingredients**

8 small potatoes, peeled; a generous pinch of saffron; 1 tbsp of parsley leaves, finely chopped; extra-virgin olive oil; salt

**Method**

Using a sharp knife, cut each potato into an egg shape. Bring a pan of water to the boil and add the saffron and a pinch of salt, then add the potatoes and lower the heat to allow the potatoes to simmer for 15 minutes, until tender. Once done, drain the potatoes, then sprinkle over the parsley, a drizzle of olive oil and a pinch of salt and serve.

Artichoke season brings about a hurried rewriting of tapas menus throughout Spain as the country welcomes this king of vegetables. For a few months, artichokes are gastronomically trending – fried with garlic, pickled in lemon juice and pink peppercorns, roasted with thyme and toasted almonds, shaved and served with paper-thin *jamón* and chunks of crumbly Manchego, and as the wholesome green component in mountain paellas of rabbit and snails.

Like the very best kind of addict, I overdose on seasonality (think artichokes, calçots, wild mushrooms and white asparagus) to the point of gluttony. But who among us is able to maintain any self-control when you can count the days until the season of fresh, glorious green and purple artichokes comes to an end. Immerse yourself, give in to gluttony and save your confessions for when the seasons change and this ethereal vegetable is relegated to the tin.

# GRILLED ARTICHOKES
## WITH BROAD BEAN AND LEMON PURÉE

**45 MIN**

### Ingredients

Juice and zest of 1 lemon

4 artichokes

12 garlic cloves

2 sprigs of thyme

1 tbsp extra-virgin olive oil

340g fresh or frozen broad beans

2 tbsp of parsley leaves, roughly chopped

2 tsp sweet paprika

Salt and cracked black pepper

### Method

Preheat the oven to 180°C/Gas Mark 4. Set aside a bowl filled with cold water and add two thirds of the lemon juice. Peel the outer leaves off the artichokes and slice each one lengthways into quarters. Remove the hairy chokes, then drop the wedges into the bowl of lemony water and leave for 5 minutes. Drain the artichokes and lay them in a roasting tray, cut side up. Top with garlic cloves and thyme leaves, and drizzle over half a tablespoon of oil. Season with salt and black pepper. Transfer the tray to the oven and roast for 40 minutes, shaking occasionally and dressing with more oil if the artichokes begin to dry out.

Put the beans in a blender along with lemon zest, roasted garlic, parsley, remaining lemon juice and half a tablespoon of oil. Season with salt and pepper, then blend until smooth. Spread the bean cream on a plate then arrange the roasted artichokes on top and drizzle with a little more olive oil and dust with the sweet paprika.

109

# FROM RUSSIA WITH LOVE, AND LASHINGS OF MAYONNAISE

This salad proves that the Russian influence in Spain goes beyond the support offered to the Republican side during the civil war. The Russians left Spain with what is almost certainly the country's most popular salad (tell the locals it's a salad and they'll laugh). While communism might not have taken hold, Lucien Olivier's original combination, a mainstay of tapas bars stretching between San Sebastián and Malaga, certainly did. I tried the dish for the first time in the Costa del Sol's Alicante, where it came topped with tropical chunks of pineapple and grated hard-boiled egg.

Direct from Moscow, with the addition of creamy white asparagus and the peerless Ortiz tuna, Spain has made this potato salad its own. So I guess it's not entirely true to say, 'Don't be fooled into turning to communism looking for food,' (Jomo Kenyatta).

# RUSSIAN SALAD
## WITH ORTIZ TUNA AND WHITE ASPARAGUS

**30 MIN**

## Ingredients

1 tsp Dijon mustard

3 eggs

2 tbsp white wine vinegar

100ml extra-virgin olive oil

3 potatoes, peeled and cut into 3cm x 3cm cubes

2 carrots, peeled and cut into 3cm x 3cm cubes

150g peas

8 white or green asparagus

1 red pepper, deseeded and chopped

1 green pepper, deseeded and chopped

2 spring onions, finely chopped

300g Ortiz tuna (or any other quality tuna in olive oil)

2 tbsp capers

Smoked paprika, for garnish

## Method

First make the mayonnaise. Put the Dijon mustard with the yolk of one egg (discard the remaining egg white), white wine vinegar and salt in a pestle and mortar. Slowly add the oil, a little at a time, and continue to mix using the pestle, until the mixture is emulsified and thick, then set aside.

Boil the potatoes in salted water for 5 minutes until tender. Remove them using a slotted spoon and refresh in iced water, then drain and set aside. Turn the heat down on the potato pan then add the carrots and leave to simmer for 5 minutes until just tender. Then finally simmer the peas for 2 minutes.

Bring a small saucepan of water to the boil and add the two remaining eggs. Bring back to the boil and then turn off the heat and cover with a lid. Leave for 7 minutes, then remove the eggs with a slotted spoon. Drop them into a bowl of iced water then peel once cool and set aside. Break off the hard parts of the asparagus stalks and steam for 5 minutes until tender then refresh in iced water, slice and set aside. Mix the potatoes, carrots, peas, peppers and spring onion with the Dijon mayonnaise, then set aside.

Mound the potato-vegetable mixture in the centre of a serving plate, then top with sliced asparagus, flakes of Ortiz tuna and capers, then drizzle over a little olive oil and season with salt and pepper. Finally, grate the hard-boiled eggs over the top then dust with smoked paprika and serve with lashings of love.

**111**

FROM THE SEA

# THREE HEARTS

## MAKE FOR A WHOLE LOTTA LOVE

Do you know octopus? You might have met at a dinner party once, or perhaps at the local Greek taverna. But you don't know octopus until you've been to Galicia. The *pulpo* is the bounty of the hardened Galician fisherman, and pulled from the Atlantic tentacles and all, it is another beast entirely.

In this wild corner of Spain, *pulpo* is prepared using traditional techniques to which there are no modern shortcuts. Fishermen and chefs (most of the time they are one and the same) apply the *asustar* technique of 'scaring' the creature before submerging it in boiling water several times, then leaving it to simmer until quaveringly tender.

Gracefully hacked into rustic discs, then drizzled with thick yellow olive oil and seasoned with rock salt and *pimentón*, you've never met octopus until you've become acquainted with *pulpo a la gallega*. Get acquainted, but know that you're more than likely to fall in love with at least one of its hearts.

# PULPO A LA GALLEGA

**90** MIN

## Ingredients

1 whole frozen octopus

3 potatoes, peeled but left whole

2 tbsp capers

30ml extra-virgin olive oil

1 tsp smoked paprika

Salt

## Method

Prepare the octopus by cleaning the tentacles and body of any remaining ink under running water. Bring a large pot to the boil, then dip the frozen octopus in for 10 seconds. Remove it and wait for the water to come back to the boil, then repeat this process three times. Finally turn down the heat and leave the octopus to simmer for at least 1 hour until tender, then remove and set aside, but keep warm.

Bring the same water back to the boil, add the potatoes and simmer for 15 minutes until tender, then remove, drain and cut into 5cm-thick rounds. Arrange the potatoes on a serving plate, then cut the still-warm octopus into thick discs and arrange on top of the potato. Sprinkle with capers, drizzle with olive oil, sprinkle with smoked paprika and season with salt, then sit back and give thanks to Galicia and its fisherman.

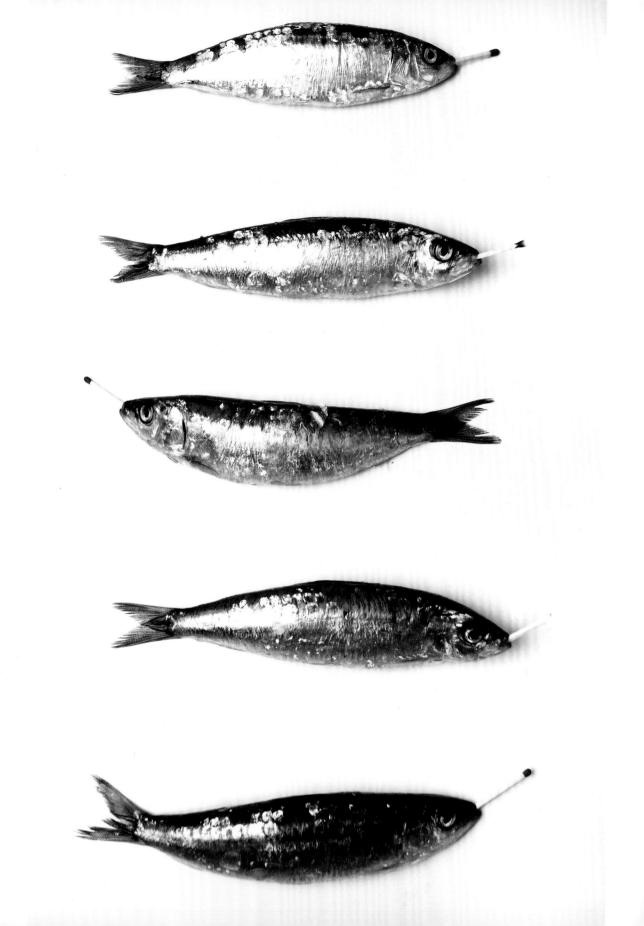

I like sardines. I eat them from the tin. I lay them on hunks of bread smeared with allioli. I buy them fresh from Montse at La Boqueria, then spear them with rosemary and grill them until their skin bubbles and blisters and their spines become soft and sweet. I am a predator of the sea. But I prefer to start at the bottom of the food chain and tend to eat the heads rather than display them in my trophy room.

It's not just a phase; I've opened cases of these silver beauties living life as a hard-up student through to my days as a suit and tie. As I mature, or at least age, I feel obliged to choose more refined offerings with fewer heads, tails and scales, but I can't imagine ever giving up this fishy vice.

In my local market, fishermen pour buckets of blue fish onto their graves of ice and I am drawn to the glint. Every creature imaginable fills this beautiful corner of the market, but I can't go past my queen of the sea. With bright eyes and a mosaic of scales, they are whole with their integrity intact. I can sense within some of them a hope that the ice will melt to form another ocean into which they can simply swim away.

Yes, you can have your crab claws, jellied eels, fleshy sashimi and egotistic snapper; your butter-poached lobster, prawn cocktail, seared scallop and moules-frites. I'll even pass on the razor clams, Rockefeller oysters and salmon confit. Just give me my Queen of the Sea. La Reina del Mar. The Sardine.

# GRILLED SARDINES
## WITH TOMATO AND PARSLEY SALAD

**15 MIN**

### Ingredients

1kg fresh sardines, cleaned and filleted (have your fishmonger
do this for you or do the job yourself; see below)
35g unblanched almonds, toasted and roughly chopped
A handful of flat-leaf parsley
Extra-virgin olive oil

Zest and juice of ½ lemon
1 tbsp capers
10 cherry tomatoes, halved
Salt

### Method

To clean and fillet the sardines, break off the heads and pull out the innards, then grab the spine with one hand and strip the sardine with the other. You should be left with a perfectly butterflied fish. Rinse and brush off any scales, then pat dry. Once dry, season the skin with plenty of salt and set aside. Use a mortar and pestle to crush the chopped almonds with parsley, olive oil and lemon zest and juice. Pound until you reach a pesto-like consistency, then stir in the capers. Put the cherry tomatoes in a bowl and stir through the pesto to coat fully. Arrange the tomatoes on a plate. Heat a lug of oil in a large frying pan and, once sizzling, add the sardines skin-side down (cook in batches to keep the pan hot). Fry the sardines for 2 minutes until the underside is golden, then flip and fry the other side for just 10 seconds more, then remove from the pan. Lay the sardines on the dressed tomatoes, then drizzle with a little more oil, and season with a pinch of salt. Serve with a wedge of lemon.

Pasta is one dish that Spain has embraced and now calls its own. But not the pedestrian spaghetti or the comforting macaroni; I'm talking about fideuà. I don't say this is my top pasta dish lightly. I remember breakfasts of stock-soaked noodles on the streets of Singapore, my first taste of *spaghetti alle vongole* in Rome and the silky lasagne served up in New York's Little Italy.

But fideuà wins out. Short like twigs, these golden eggy noodles are fried in olive oil, then cooked in a salty shellfish stock with chunks of white fish, juicy squid and red Palamos prawns, and then topped with dollops of black squid-ink allioli. You can't help but agree with Federico Fellini that 'life is a combination of magic and pasta', even in rice-loving Spain.

# FIDEUÀ
## WITH SQUID INK ALLIOLI

**40** MIN

### Ingredients

2 tbsp allioli (see page 17)

1 tsp black squid ink (you can buy these as frozen sachets from the supermarket)

4 tbsp extra-virgin olive oil

500g monkfish (or other firm white fish), chopped into chunks

300g squid, chopped into chunks

500g fideuà (broken spaghetti will do if you can't find fideuà)

1 tbsp sweet paprika

1 litre seafood fumet (see page 27)

300g raw king prawns

1 lemon, cut into 4 wedges

A small handful of flat-leaf parsley

Salt and cracked black pepper

### Method

Put the allioli in a small bowl and add the squid ink. Mix until fully combined to a ghoulish black. Next, heat a lug of oil in a large saucepan over a high heat. Season the chunks of monkfish and add to the pan. Fry for 5 minutes until golden, then remove with a slotted spoon and set aside. Add the squid to the same pan and repeat the process. Then add the fideuà to the empty pan with some more oil and a pinch of the sweet paprika, then fry for a few minutes until the pasta is coated in the oil and beginning to sizzle. Add the fumet and return the fish and squid to the pan and simmer until the liquid has reduced by half. Finally, arrange the prawns around the edge of the pan and leave to cook, until all the liquid has evaporated and the fideuà is al dente. Remove the pan from the heat and cover with a tea towel. Leave covered for 5 minutes.

Serve the fideuà with dollops of black allioli, lemon wedges and freshly chopped parsley. Pour yourself a glass of something cold and white and clink glasses with the world.

I first came across trout in a nature documentary, in which David Attenborough, in his soothing, dulcet tones, described the savage fate of Canadian trout as they swam upstream into the waiting mouths of big brown bears.

Seeing the same fish relaxing in the markets of Barcelona leads me to believe that the Spanish lifestyle flowed all the way into the Mediterranean sea. As a Spanish trout you have a good life; there is no swimming upstream, there are no bears, and you'll meet your fate in a most delicious way. And with worms being hard to find in Spain, fishermen resort to prawn *escabeche* and baby calamari to hook their catch. Neither the trout nor discerning gourmets are any match for such temptation.

# TROUT WITH ALMOND PICADA, JAMÓN, THYME AND ORANGE

**30 MIN**

### Ingredients

70g unblanched almonds, toasted

1 bunch of thyme sprigs, leaves picked

1 egg yolk

30ml extra-virgin olive oil, plus extra for dressing

4 tbsp apple cider vinegar

2 oranges; one zested, the other sliced

4 medium-sized trout

4 slices of jamón

1 lemon, cut into 4 wedges

Salt

### Method

Preheat the oven to 180°C/Gas Mark 4. Using a mortar and pestle, pound the toasted almonds with some thyme, the egg yolk, olive oil, apple cider vinegar and orange zest into a paste, then set aside.

Prepare each trout by slicing along the belly under the head, removing the innards, washing under cold water, then patting dry. Place the trout in a baking dish, open out and fill each with the almond paste, then add the jamón, orange slices and more thyme. Close the trout and season the skins with salt, then bake in the oven for 10 minutes until the skin is beginning to crisp and the flesh is pink and flaky.

To serve, dress with more fresh thyme leaves, a drizzle of olive oil, salt and a wedge of lemon.

# A TIE IS THE FIRST SERIOUS STEP IN LIFE

The day I saw salmon in the same list as chia seeds, coconut oil, goji berries and kefir I knew the fish was doomed to life in the murky mainstream. Like the best kind of marketing, 'superfoods' made us feel like pioneers as we casually tried to detect and enjoy the new flavours that promised us superpowers. But salmon is a no-brainer: it is luscious and meaty with none of the fishiness that the precious among us won't stand for.

Travel to Japan and you witness a truly deep love for the pink-fleshed beauty. Nothing will compare to the salmon sashimi I tasted at Tsukiji market before the sun was up. Burly, yet somehow graceful Japanese fishermen mixed with cut-throat black-suited vendors and the city's top chefs. It was as close to chaos as Japan gets. There I stood, shivering in the cavernous shed as huge beasts of the sea were hauled onto the auction floor and acquired for thousands of yen. With this profound experience top of my mind, my daily sashimi routine in the dark in the curtained restaurants of Shinjuku or neon-lit bars of Tokyo's awesome subway suddenly stood for something more than longevity and perfect skin.

# CRISPY SALMON
## WITH SALSA VERDE AND WHITE BEANS

**40 MIN**

### Ingredients

200g dry white beans
3 bay leaves
2 tbsp salsa verde (see page 23)
4 salmon fillets
20ml extra-virgin olive oil
2 tbsp capers
Salt and cracked black pepper

### Method

Soak the beans overnight. Boil them in the morning with the bay leaves until tender, then strain. Tip the hot beans into a bowl, add the salsa verde and toss to coat.

Brush the skin of the salmon fillets with oil, then season with salt and cracked black pepper. Heat the oil (reserving a little for dressing) in a large frying pan and once hot, add the salmon, skin-side down. Fry for 5 minutes, until the skin is golden and crispy, then flip the salmon and fry for just another minute or two, depending on how you like it cooked.

Divide the beans equally between four plates, then top each portion with a salmon fillet. Drizzle over a little olive oil and top with dollops of salsa verde. Finally, scatter capers over the top for a salty crunch.

Baby squid are available all year round in Spain but are at their sweetest in late July. They are beautiful creatures, with their smooth white opaque flesh coated in a dark black membrane. If you are lucky enough to get them fresh, their ink sacs of pure melanin will still be attached, offering amino acids as well as the pure flavour of the deep sea. The ink and the squid go together in the ocean, as they should on the plate – black and white, perfect in their contrast.

# BABY SQUID FILLED WITH BLACK RICE AND PINE NUTS

**90 MIN**

## Ingredients

4 baby squid, cleaned and tentacles and ink sac separated

2 squid ink sachets, diluted in 400ml of water (you can get these frozen from speciality stores)

260ml white wine

Extra-virgin olive oil

2 onions, chopped

2 garlic cloves

1 bay leaf

3 tomatoes, diced

200g Arborio rice

10 prawns, peeled, deveined and finely chopped

50g pine nuts, toasted

Peel and wedges of 1 lemon

Salt and cracked black pepper

## Method

Preheat the grill to medium. If preparing the squid yourself, peel off the dark membrane and remove the tentacles, then slice out the ink sacs and dilute the contents in 200ml of water. Mix the inky liquid with 60ml white wine, then set aside.

Heat a lug of oil in a large saucepan over a high heat. When hot, add the onions, garlic and bay leaf, season with salt and black pepper, and fry for 10 minutes until the onions have softened and turned translucent. Add the rice, then fry for 10 minutes, stirring the pan regularly. Add the inky liquid and simmer for a further 15 minutes until the liquid has evaporated and the rice is cooked al dente. Add the chopped prawns and toasted pine nuts and stir to combine.

Place a separate large frying pan over a high heat and heat a lug of oil to sizzling. Add the squid bodies and fry until golden on all sides. Remove the squid from the pan using a slotted spoon and set aside. Preheat the oven to 180°C/Gas Mark 4. Fill each squid body with inky rice, using toothpicks to hold the squid together, and set aside any leftover rice. Place the squid rolls in a small baking dish and pour over the remaining wine. Add the lemon peel to the wine and place the dish in the oven to bake for 1 hour. To serve, drizzle with olive oil, season with salt and serve with a wedge of lemon.

I never went to culinary school. No one ever taught me how to make a classic *beurre noisette* or a wobbly panna cotta, or the correct technique to break down and fillet animals. But I made up for the lack of technical training with a resilient ego and non-stop kitchen experiments. If I *had* made it to Cordon Bleu or a similar institution, there is one master I would have bowed down to: Michel Roux Jr. This rockstar chef runs marathons (shared pain brings people together), but he also has a deep respect for tradition and the fundamentals. Even though we never shared a chopping board, via YouTube he taught me that pure flavours and simplicity are always trending. One of his signature dishes is mackerel *escabeche*, a traditional preparation that uses acid to cut through the natural oiliness of this super fish. I gave it a Spanish-flavoured slap around the face, with the words of Roux Jr, 'Every chef has to know the classics', ringing in my ears.

# ESCABECHE
## WITH PICKLED VEGETABLES, TOASTED SEEDS AND SPICES

**90 MIN**

### Ingredients

2 mackerel
2 tbsp extra-virgin olive oil
65ml sherry vinegar
130ml apple cider vinegar
Peel of ½ a lemon
4 black peppercorns
1 bay leaf

5 raisins
6 thyme sprigs, leaves picked
2 shallots, finely sliced
2 carrots, sliced with a
   microplane
5–10 baby radishes, sliced with
   a microplane

1 apple (such as Granny Smith),
   cored and sliced with a
   microplane
1 tbsp coriander seeds, toasted
2 tbsp sunflower seeds, toasted
Salt

### Method

Prepare mackerel by removing head and intestines, scaling, then carefully separating fillet from spine with a sharp knife. Pat dry and sprinkle salt over the skin. Heat a lug of oil in a frying pan over a medium heat. Add the mackerel fillets, skin-side down, and fry until the undersides are golden, then flip and fry for another 10 seconds. Remove the mackerel from the pan and set aside, skin-side up. Bring the sherry vinegar to a simmer, then add the apple cider vinegar, lemon peel, black peppercorns, bay leaf, raisins, thyme and finely sliced shallots. Simmer for 5 minutes, then add carrots and cook for a further 5 minutes until the carrots soften. Finally, add the radish and apple slices, cook for 1 minute and remove from heat. Tip the mixture into a deep dish and then carefully add the mackerel, skin-side up, so that the marinade covers all the flesh. Place the dish in the fridge for at least 1 hour to cure.

Take the mackerel out of the fridge, remove from the marinade and pat dry. Slice into wedges (feel free to remove the skin or leave it for a nice silvery visual). Arrange the mackerel slices and the mixture of sliced apple, carrots, shallots and radishes on a plate, then sprinkle with the toasted seeds, drizzle with oil, season with salt and serve.

# NOT ALL
# TREASURE IS SILVER
# AND GOLD, MATE,

My two best friends (anyone from school you still call a friend 10 years later rightfully deserves this label) live on the other side of the world, but what do they say about distance and the heart?

We used to spend summers at a small beach town in southern Tasmania learning how to get drunk, swimming in a shark-infested bay, and taking turns at displaying our skills with tongs and a BBQ. We also searched the bay for treasures: reeling in baby squid, baby snapper and perch from the jetty, then diving deep for big white shells filled with plump abalone and scallops.

Back then summers were never-ending (although they don't feel that short these days either) and they provide an endless supply of memories. In that remote bay we scouted and devoured a bounty of delicate white-shelled molluscs, together with blackened sausages and charred onions and the cheapest ketchup on sale at the solitary local store. Those days were golden and no matter how much time passes, I know that bay and those friendships will never change.

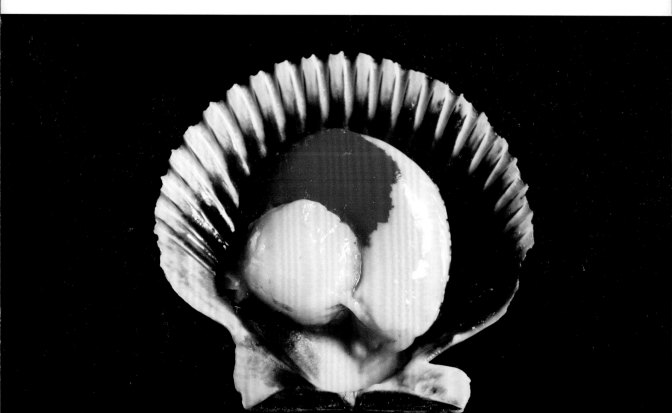

# CRISPY SCALLOPS
## ON SAFFRON PURÉE WITH JAMÓN SHARDS

### Ingredients

½ a head of cauliflower, broken into florets
Zest and juice of ½ a lemon
Extra-virgin olive oil
1 shallot, chopped
1 garlic clove, crushed
A pinch of saffron threads
2 thyme sprigs, leaves picked
75g almonds, blanched and peeled
16 large scallops, roe removed (keep the shells for presentation)
6 jamón slices
Salt and cracked black pepper

**30 MIN**

### Method

Bring a large saucepan of water to the boil, then reduce the heat to a simmer and cook the cauliflower for 5–8 minutes, until tender. Drain, squeeze the lemon juice over the top and set aside. Heat a lug of oil in a large saucepan. Add the shallot and garlic and fry for 5 minutes. Add the saffron, most of the thyme leaves and cauliflower and fry for a further 10 minutes, until the shallots are sweet and sticky. Scrape everything into a blender along with the almonds. Season with salt and pepper and whizz with 3–4 tablespoons of oil until smooth.

Wash the scallops and pat dry, then season both sides with salt. Heat a lug of oil in a frying pan and, once hot, fry the scallops for 2–3 minutes until golden on the underside, then flip and fry for an additional minute, so that they are still translucent in the centre. Remove and set aside.

Heat the grill to medium. Fill the empty scallop shells with the cauliflower purée, then top with the scallop, torn jamón and the rest of the thyme leaves. Place on a baking tray and finish off under the grill until the jamón crisps up, then remove and serve still hot.

135

# WITH A STREET VALUE RIVALLING COCAINE, SAFFRON IS STRAIGHT OUTTA SPAIN

My grandmother, Josette (she will always be Mamama to me) grew up in Catalonia before following my Swiss grandfather to Bern, a city that contrasted the brash colour and unashamed pride of Barcelona with a careful and measured Swiss exactness. Her new geography influenced her cooking and left me with memories of toasted flour soup, sausages and potatoes, bircher muesli, vermicelli chestnut cream, and, of course, untold amounts of Swiss chocolate. But she did retain one dish inspired by the Mediterranean.

I've added a few extra touches to her Saffron Fish, combining a deep seafood *fumet* with orange, star anise and the reliable magic of saffron. As Rémy of *Ratatouille* fame said as he called on saffron to save Linguini's sauce, 'Anyone can cook ... but only the fearless can be great', and this exotic spice helps anyone be great.

# SAFFRON FISH

40 MIN

### Ingredients

2 tbsp extra-virgin olive oil

5 shallots, finely chopped

1 bay leaf

2–3 thyme sprigs, leaves picked

1 star anise

Peel of ½ an orange

A pinch of saffron

500ml white wine

120ml single cream

4 white fish fillets (such as cod), skins removed

Salt

### Method

Preheat the oven to 180°C/Gas Mark 4. Heat a lug of oil in a medium pan. Add the shallots, bay leaf and thyme. Season, then fry until the onion begins to soften. Add the star anise, orange peel, saffron and white wine, then reduce the heat and simmer until the mixture begins to thicken (about 15 minutes). Taste and adjust the seasoning, then add the cream and simmer to reduce until the sauce coats the back of a spoon (about 15 minutes). Strain through a fine sieve and set the liquid aside.

Lay the fish fillets in a baking dish, then pour over the saffron sauce. Place the dish in a hot oven and bake for 15 minutes, until the sauce begins to bubble and turn golden. Serve with crusty bread and steamed potatoes or simple rice to soak up all the delicious saffron nectar.

It took God to bring *bacallà* to the world via the Benedictine monks, who stretched insufficient supplies of cod by salting and drying it for use over the cold bleak winters, when the Mediterranean sea rebuffed any attempts to steal its bounty.

I first came across *bacallà* at La Boqueria market in my first week living in Barcelona. I stutteringly ordered with my dismal Spanish and returned home with a fillet of *bacallà* belly meat – glistening with salt and wrapped in paper like the best kind of gift. The simmering heat of August in Barcelona demanded *esqueixada* and it was a revelation. A close cousin of *ceviche*, the dish gave way to a rich butteriness that made me proud that even just one quarter of my blood is Catalan.

Look beyond the salty exterior of *bacallà* and, like the hardened exteriors of local Catalans, you will discover a flavour that is naturally sweet and deeply nourishing.

# ESQUEIXADA
## WITH TOMATO CONSOMMÉ, BLACK OLIVE OIL AND BABY HERBS

**30 MIN**

### Ingredients

2 large bacallà fillets
1 red pepper, deseeded and finely chopped
1 yellow pepper, deseeded and finely chopped
4 tbsp extra-virgin olive oil
10 ripe tomatoes
1 beetroot, chopped

10ml sherry vinegar
5 tbsp torn basil leaves
30g black Spanish olives, chopped
1 orange, peeled, segmented and finely chopped
2 tbsp capers

### Method

Prepare the bacallà by soaking and refreshing in water four times over two days. Once ready, gently tear into small strips and mix with half the chopped pepper and 2 tablespoons of olive oil, then set aside.

Prepare the consommé: blend the tomatoes with beetroot, remaining red and yellow pepper, vinegar and most of the basil until smooth, then strain through a muslin cloth. Place the chopped olives in a bowl with 2 tablespoons of olive oil and use a stick blender to whizz until smooth. Strain the liquid to make a black olive oil.

Place the bacallà in the base of a bowl, then pour consommé around it, top with chopped orange and capers, then drizzle with a little black olive oil and decorate with baby basil leaves.

Learning how to cook rice is a rite-of-passage in Spain. For me, María-Angeles Alberich, who turned ninety last year, was my guru. This timelessly beautiful old lady lives in sunny Torredembarra and, since moving to Spain, I have formed a bond with her that extends beyond the rice, *fideuà* and fresh fish lunches that formed the basis of our relationship. On one visit, she chose *arroz verde* (green rice) as the dish of the day. I took the first train from Barcelona and an hour later, after a quick swim at the beach on arrival, I was in position with an empty notebook and camera ready to capture, cook and eat.

I still visit this inspirational woman whose stories of being a model in Barcelona and owning the city's first red convertible are not hard to believe as I watch her walk with poise and elegance along the beach, stopping occasionally to pick up shells that always seem to end up taped to letters and poking out of my mailbox. She will always be my Spanish godmother and someone who gave my cooking soul and my food a personality.

# GREEN ALMOND RICE COOKED IN FUMET WITH GRILLED MUSSELS

**30 MIN**

## Ingredients

Extra-virgin olive oil
200g squid, chopped into chunks
4 garlic cloves
2½ small bunches of parsley
2 green peppers, deseeded and chopped

370g white or brown short-grain rice
1 litre seafood fumet (see page 27)
4 tbsp breadcrumbs
Zest of 1 lemon

300g mussels
250ml white wine
Wedge of lemon
Salt and cracked black pepper

## Method

Heat a lug of oil in a large saucepan, then add the squid and a pinch of salt and fry for 5 minutes until golden. Remove the pan from heat and set the squid aside. Peel and chop 3 garlic cloves and add to a food processor with 1 bunch of parsley, green pepper and 2–3 tablespoons of olive oil. Season with salt and pepper, then blend to a fine texture. Add more oil to the pan, then gently fry the pepper mix until beginning to soften. Add the rice and some more oil and stir until all grains are well coated. Add ¾ of the fumet, then lower the heat and simmer for 30 minutes until the liquid has reduced. Add the remaining fumet, then return the squid to the pan and simmer over a low heat until the liquid has reduced again.

Mix 1 more bunch of finely chopped parsley with the remaining clove of chopped garlic, breadcrumbs and lemon zest. Season and stir together to form a rough crumb then set aside. Under running water, remove beards and any grit from the mussels. Heat the wine in a large pan over a medium heat. Once simmering, add the mussels and cover with the lid. As soon as mussels are beginning to open, remove the pan from the stove and discard any empty mussel shells, keeping those that have mussels attached.

Heat the grill to hot. Spread the rice in a baking dish, then top with the mussel shells you have kept. Sprinkle over the breadcrumb mixture, dress with olive oil and season with salt and pepper. Place under a hot grill for 5–10 minutes until the crust is golden. Sprinkle with the remaining ½ bunch of parsley and serve with a wedge of lemon.

The tuna, depending on its hue, is destined for the rich man's platter of sashimi or the poor man's tin (class divisions stretch beyond the sea). Bonito is not tuna. For me it is the stylish and wilder ocean cousin. Silvery blue skin covering fleshy salty meat and a flavour that will make you shrug your shoulders when you catch glimpses of pornographic plates of red tuna belly. The bonito oozes distinction and a modesty that demands similarly simple accompaniments. No edible flowers or micro herbs here, just a thick dollop of punchy allioli and baked potatoes – real food to honour a real fish.

# BONITO BAKED WITH BLACK OLIVES, GREEN PEPPERS AND ALLIOLI

**30 MIN**

## Ingredients

1 onion, sliced into rings

100g black Spanish olives

1 tbsp extra-virgin olive oil

2 tbsp allioli (see page 17)

2 green peppers, deseeded and sliced

4 bonito fillets (buy skipjack tuna, or replace with mackerel)

1 lemon, cut into wedges, to serve

Salt and cracked black pepper

## Method

Preheat the oven to 180°C/Gas Mark 4. Arrange the onion slices on a baking tray. Sprinkle over the olives, then drizzle over 1 tablespoon of olive oil and a spoonful of allioli, and season with salt and black pepper. Lay the bonito fillets on top, then top with the pepper slices and spread the remaining allioli over the top. Bake for 15–20 minutes until the fish is cooked to your liking and the allioli is beginning to turn golden and form a crust. Serve the bonito on a bed of the roasted onion and olive mixture with a wedge of lemon and a view of the ocean (use a screensaver if this reality isn't possible).

FROM THE LAND

# WHEN IT COMES TO LAMB I ALWAYS PREFER A LEG

New Zealand is famous for a few things: a hulking team of All Blacks, one of the most progressive and positive relationships with the country's indigenous people, the Maori, devastating nature (*Lord of the Rings* didn't really require CGI when it came to filming the landscapes), and sheep.

It doesn't matter how far I stray from the land of the long white cloud, everyone always has a joke about the Kiwi love affair with wool. And it's true – show me a slender lamb leg in purple shoes and I swoon. Combine it with dark silvery anchovies, garlicky allioli, the fresh bite of green olives and rosemary, and I enter a fleece-induced weakening of the knees. Maybe it's because New Zealand and Spain celebrate sheep and lamb in the kitchen so seriously that I announce with such pride my ties to both nations.

# LAMB SHANKS
## AND POTATOES BAKED WITH ANCHOVIES
## AND PARSLEY GREMOLATA

**120 MIN**

### Ingredients

1 leg of lamb (approx. 2–3kg)

40ml extra-virgin olive oil

6 rosemary sprigs, leaves picked and finely chopped

2 green peppers, finely chopped

4 tbsp parsley, leaves picked

3 garlic cloves, finely chopped

1 tsp capers

Zest of ½ lemon and juice of 1 whole

2 bay leaves

1 tbsp of fennel seeds

4 potatoes, roughly cut, skin left on

10–15 anchovies

2 onions, finely chopped

100g green olives, pitted

400ml dry white wine

3 tbsp allioli (see page 17)

Salt and cracked black pepper

### Method

Rub the lamb all over with the oil, then season with salt and pepper. Rub 3 sprigs of rosemary leaves all over the meat and place the lamb in the fridge for 20 minutes. Meanwhile, prepare the gremolata by mixing the green peppers with the parsley, garlic, capers, lemon zest and juice, bay leaves and fennel seeds. Season with salt and pepper. And mix again.

Preheat the oven to 180°C/Gas Mark 4. Spread the gremolata over the base of the baking dish then arrange the potatoes, anchovies, onions, olives and 3 sprigs of rosemary leaves and pour over the wine. Lay the lamb on top and slather the whole thing with beautiful, beautiful allioli (holding just a little back for later). Transfer to the oven and bake for 1 hour 15 minutes for tender, pink lamb. Remove from the oven, cover and allow to rest for 15 minutes before serving in thin slices with another heap of allioli for the garlic addicts out there.

Much to my father's disappointment, I missed my graduation ceremony – no scrolls or gowns for me. Instead, I took the first flight out of Tasmania to chase corporate dreams tied in double Windsor knots.

Life at my new job in Melbourne was everything I hoped for. I spent my days in front of Excel sheets crunching numbers, joined every other grey-suited clone at lunchtime sushi trains, and explored the city at night. Along with discovering the winding Yarra River that linked the city with the bush, and the graffiti that gave me a reason to enter every dark alley around the city, I found the celebrated tapas bar MoVida.

My first visit to Frank Camorra's original Melbourne offering was unforgettable. To this day I can remember the *pà amb tomàquet* (wafer thin toast, olive oil caviar, tomato sorbet and a simple Ortiz anchovy; see page 43), the mushrooms in Pedro Ximenez sherry, the lamb kidneys braised in smoked paprika, and of course, the crackable *crema Catalana*.

MoVida dragged me away from the foams, gels and edible soils that Melbourne was in those days celebrating, and back to the real food that my subconscious knew represented Spain. Camorra's food, and general philosophy, continues to inspire locals to visit Spain and, in some lucky cases, remain there for life.

# CHICKEN BRAISED IN SHERRY VINEGAR GRAPES
## WITH

**60** MIN

## Ingredients

4 large chicken drumsticks

30ml extra-virgin olive oil

1 onion, chopped

2 garlic cloves, chopped

2 thyme sprigs

2 bay leaves

120g sherry vinegar, plus extra to serve

120g chicken caldo (see recipe on page 25)

2 tbsp cream

150g green grapes, halved and deseeded

A handful flat-leaf parsley, leaves shredded

A handful of almonds, toasted and chopped

Salt and cracked black pepper

## Method

Season the chicken drumsticks with salt and pepper. Heat a pan with oil then add the drumsticks and fry until they begin to brown on all sides. Remove with a slotted spoon and set aside. Add some more oil to the pan then add the onion, garlic, thyme and bay leaves. Season with a pinch of salt and pepper over a low heat for 15 minutes, until onions begin to turn golden. Return the chicken to the pan and add the sherry vinegar and chicken caldo. Braise over a low heat, turning the drumsticks regularly. After 30 minutes, as the sauce begins to thicken, add the cream and stir through. Finally, add the grapes, then leave to reduce for 10 minutes, until the sauce becomes syrupy. Arrange the chicken on a plate and top with the onion and grape sauce, then sprinkle over the parsley and almonds and finish off with a splash of sherry vinegar.

151

No sane child ever has good memories of lentils, but I grew up in a house where the tiny brown pulse was a weekly feature at the table. My mother flavoured our lentils with rosemary, lemon, and other perfectly valid flavours that only a seven-year-old wouldn't appreciate. With my father's generational expectations that plates would always be finished, I knew drastic measures were necessary. So, sneaking back to the kitchen, I quietly pulled out the bright red ketchup bottle, slid the nozzle under my heap of lentils, and squeezed. I sat back down with what appeared to be the original plate and carried on shovelling from plate to mouth, catching a smear of the toxic sauce on every forkful. Desperate times, desperate measures.

I've matured, at least my palate has, and as an early adopter, I now pass by gastro-pubs and hip bistros for whom the lentil is a regular feature and smile knowingly. If only they knew that there is no need for accompaniments like confit chicken, charred lamb or grilled snapper. Sit me in the corner with a plate of steaming lentils and a bottle of cheap ketchup and I'll lick the plate clean.

# BAKED LENTILS WITH MORCILLA CRUST AND SALSA VERDE

**45 MIN**

## Ingredients

50g breadcrumbs

Zest of 1 lemon

3 rosemary sprigs, 1 whole and the others leaves picked and finely chopped

4 garlic cloves, crushed (one kept separate)

300g brown lentils

3 bay leaves

50ml extra-virgin olive oil

2 thyme sprigs

1 onion, finely chopped

2 celery stalks, chopped

2 carrots, chopped

2 tomatoes, chopped

50ml white wine

150g morcilla (or any fatty cured meat), finely chopped

4 tbsp salsa verde (see page 23)

Salt and cracked black pepper

## Method

Mix the breadcrumbs with the lemon zest, rosemary leaves and 1 clove of garlic and set aside. Rinse the lentils in cold water. Put 1.5 litres of water in a large saucepan, tip in the lentils, add a bay leaf and bring to the boil. Reduce the heat and leave to simmer for 20–30 minutes until the lentils are al dente (add more water as necessary).

Heat the grill to medium. Heat oil in a pan and add the remaining bay leaves, garlic, sprigs of rosemary and the thyme, the onion, celery and carrots. Season with salt and pepper. Once the onions are beginning to soften, add the tomatoes and wine and fry until the liquid has reduced and the vegetables are just cooked. Add the lentils to the pan with some more olive oil and stir through. Transfer the lot to a baking dish and top with morcilla and the breadcrumb mixture, then drizzle with oil and heat under the grill until the crust turns golden. Serve immediately with lashings of salsa verde.

# I PROMISE
# EASTER WILL NOT
# BE CANCELLED

I grew up on a remote windswept island where local animals went by names like Tasmanian Devil and Tasmanian Tiger, a frightening contrast from the dangers of Spain, namely the mountain goat.

I am part of a family that, apart from two beautiful sisters, has included sheep, hens, pigs, ducks, goats, geese and rabbits – both pets and wild animals that bounded across our paddocks and hid in the surrounding hills. Never once did I think of eating these magical creatures until after I had left this idyllic setting and found myself in the foodie scene of hip Melbourne, where for a while the floppy-eared creature headlined menus. Rabbit, though difficult to master, is one of my favourite meats, reminding me of both the lush green fields of a Tasmanian winter and the golden hay that wilted under its scorching southern January sun. Post-Easter, the cotton-tail is a worthy sacrifice for your plate.

# RABBIT BAKED IN A SAFFRON AND ALMOND PICADA

**45** MIN

## Ingredients

35g almonds, toasted

4 garlic cloves, sliced thinly

Zest of ½ orange

A pinch of saffron threads

2 tbsp flat-leaf parsley leaves, plus extra to serve

50ml extra-virgin olive oil

2 sprigs rosemary leaves, picked and finely chopped

1 rabbit, jointed into pieces (your butcher can do this for you)

2 tomatoes, chopped

5–10 thyme sprigs

2 bay leaves

240ml dry white wine

2 tbsp sherry vinegar

10 prunes

120ml single cream

1 lemon, cut into 4 wedges

Salt and cracked black pepper

## Method

For the picada, use a mortar and pestle to crush the almonds with half the garlic, the orange zest, saffron threads and parsley. Add 2–3 tablespoons of olive oil to make a paste and season with salt and pepper. In a separate bowl, mix together 2 tablespoons of oil, the rosemary and a little salt and pepper. Rub into the rabbit pieces and leave to marinate for 10 minutes. Heat a glug of oil in a large saucepan over a high heat and, once hot, add the rabbit pieces. Fry until golden on all sides (about 10 minutes), then remove with a slotted spoon and set aside. To the same pan, add the remaining garlic, tomatoes, thyme and bay leaves, season with salt and pepper and fry until caramelized. Add the wine and sherry vinegar and let the sauce bubble away until reduced by half then add the picada (almond mixture) and prunes and braise for 10 minutes. Meanwhile, preheat the oven to 150°C/Gas Mark 2. Finally, add the cream, lower the heat and cook until sauce thickens. Place the rabbit in a baking dish and pour the sauce over the top, then bake for 15 minutes until tender and the sauce has fully reduced. Serve the rabbit sprinkled with parsley and lemon wedges on the side.

*MasterChef* was an experience – no more and no less. I made a name for myself by perfecting the poached egg, and also for slicing more fingers than onions. My fifteen minutes of fame remains a vivid memory: I recall cooking in shiny kitchens as producers called for tears and tantrums, and watching celebrity judges nervously eye off what they would eventually have to taste. In a knife-skills challenge, my three bowls of perfectly chopped onions took on a disturbing blood-red hue as I hacked my way into the bottom ten and an elimination cook-off. Along with nine other survivors, we raced into 'the pantry' to grab the bare essentials necessary to cook the 'most important dish of our lives'. I decided on this Andaluz-inspired tapa and set about translating an idea into a dish. But I somehow found myself disconcertingly calm in a setting where the crazed and crying were celebrated. It was bubblegum fun that taught me to swear loudly, and to break at least one plate any time a camera enters the kitchen. As one judge put it, 'More footy [aggression], less yoga [Zen]'.

# SAFFRON PULLED CHICKEN WITH BLACKENED CREAMED CORN AND POACHED EGG

**40 MIN**

## Ingredients

325ml dry white wine
1 bay leaf
Peel of ½ lemon
1 star anise
5 black peppercorns

2 chicken breasts
2 tbsp raisins
3 tbsp extra-virgin olive
   oil
1 tsp of smoked paprika

2 tbsp fresh parsley,
   finely chopped
120ml single cream
14 (½g) saffron threads
2 corn cobs

1 tsp white vinegar
4 eggs
Salt and cracked black
   pepper

## Method

Put the wine, bay leaf, lemon peel, star anise and peppercorns in a large saucepan. Put the pan over a high heat and heat until simmering, then add the chicken breasts and cover with a lid. Bring the liquid back to a simmer and poach for 15 minutes until cooked through and tender. Remove the chicken from the pan and tear into small strips while still hot. Coat the chicken in the raisins, olive oil, smoked paprika and parsley and season with salt and pepper, then leave to marinate.

Pour the cream and 10 of the saffron threads into a small saucepan and heat over a low heat for 5–10 minutes. Brush the corn with oil and season with salt and black pepper, then place under a hot grill, turning regularly until beginning to blacken. Slice the kernels off the cob and transfer them to a food processor with a lug of olive oil, salt and pepper and the infused cream, and blend until smooth. For the poached egg, add a dash of vinegar to a pan of simmering water. Crack the eggs into 4 individual small bowls. Using a spoon, stir the water in circles to create a whirlpool, then gently lower the first egg into the centre of the whirlpool. Leave to cook for 3 minutes, then using a slotted spoon, remove the egg and drain on kitchen paper. Repeat until you have poached all the eggs. Spoon the creamed corn onto a plate, then add the shredded chicken and top with the poached egg. Carefully place 1 strand of saffron on each poached egg so the deep colour begins to bleed, then cut through the yolk for your own self-saucing plate of delicious reality.

# SWEETS

# SENDING SUGAR OVERSEAS IS WHERE LOVE IS TRULY DEFINED

Christmas in Catalonia brings with it one slightly disturbing tradition known as 'Caga Tió' (Google it) and another, which is a sweet tooth's wet dream: *turrón*. With similarities to the Levantine halva, *turrón* has a base of honey, sugar, ground nuts and egg white that is then flavoured with toasted nuts, glacé fruit and chocolate. The crunchy Catala D'Agramunt variety was my favourite as a child, and every Christmas I trusted in the global postal system to ensure my grandparents' valuable parcel safely made its way to the other side of the world.

Upon arrival, brown boxes covered in stickers, glitter and ribbons were hastily torn open to reveal a bounty of chocolate advent calendars, crude Catalan cartoons and, most importantly, bricks of *turrón*. They never lasted long, courtesy of my sisters and (mostly) me gorging on it in a post-Christmas sugar frenzy. These days it is me sending back boxes of Spanish treats while trying, and failing, to understand and truly love Caga Tió.

Skype and the spontaneous postcard are great, but sending sugar overseas is the true definition of love.

# TURRÓN ICE CREAM
## WITH GREEN GRAPES

**6 HR 15 MIN**

Turrón de Xixona (soft *turrón* from Valencia – soft nougat can also work), chopped finely
175ml cava (sparkling white wine is fine, too)
500ml whipping cream
5 tbsp icing sugar
Zest of ½ orange
6 egg whites
Pinch of cinnamon
Turrón d'Agramunt (hard turrón from Catalonia – use crunchy nougat if you can't find it), smashed into chunks
1 tbsp honey (any kind)
1 bunch of green grapes

### Method

To make the ice cream, mix the Turrón de Xixona with the cava to form a smooth paste. In a separate bowl, beat 400ml of the cream with the icing sugar until it forms soft peaks, then fold in the turrón pieces along with the orange zest until combined.

In a separate bowl, whisk the egg whites until they form stiff peaks, then fold the creamed turrón into the whites. Pour the mixture into a plastic container and transfer to the freezer. Use a wooden spoon to beat the mixture every hour for at least 6 hours (it will form ice crystals if you just leave it; you can use an ice cream machine if you have one).

Next, add the cinnamon to the remaining 100ml of cream, and whisk until it forms soft peaks. To serve, scoop balls of the ice cream into a dessert glass, then top with the cinnamon cream, crunchy chunks of hard turrón and a drizzle of honey. Scatter the grapes over the top and dig into this decadence with small spoon that one hopes will somehow slow your gorging.

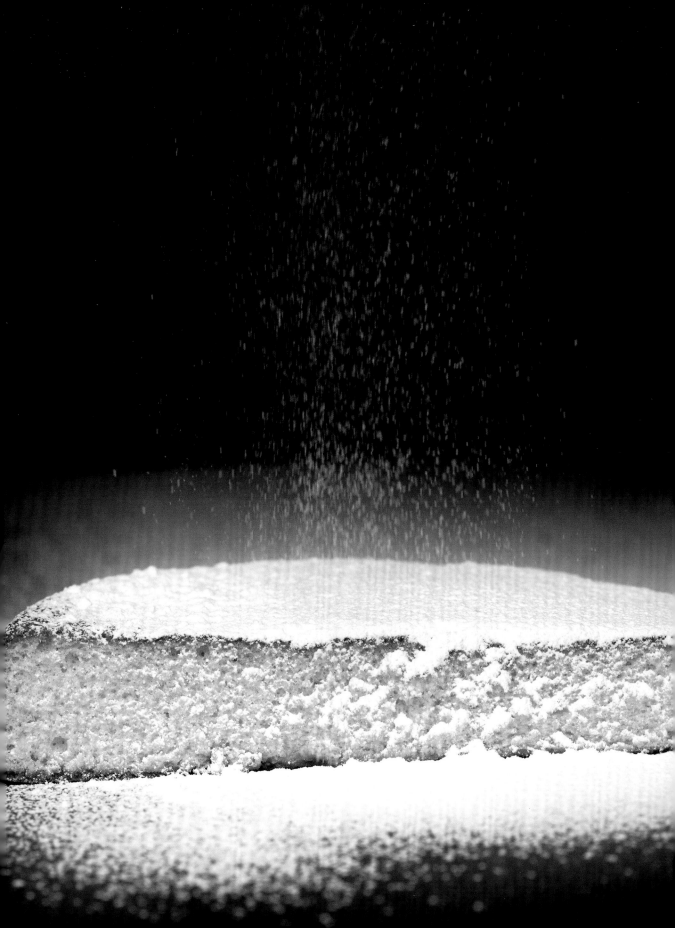

Torta de Santiago was granted cultural status by the EU in 2010 and is now required to 1) be baked in Galicia and 2) contain a minimum of 33% almonds. This is a cake that stands for something more than butter, sugar, flour and eggs.

Originating in the middle ages, the Galician tart makes short work of cakes. It is a clear winner over the buttery French galette des rois, beats hands down the revani of Turkey and Greece, easily gains ascendency over Italy's yeasty panettone, and makes the Queen Victoria sponge look like a puffed-up lightweight. Spain is surely not a threat to the northern-European baking powerhouses such as Austria and Germany, but with the Spanish lifestyle interrupting any lengthy period spent indoors, who has time to watch the oven?

# TORTA DE SANTIAGO
## WITH ORANGE AND CARDAMOM SYRUP 45 MIN

### Ingredients

| | | |
|---|---|---|
| 6 large eggs, separated | 4 drops almond extract | 4 cardamom pods |
| 200g caster sugar | 210g ground almonds | 1 tbsp olive oil |
| Zest of 1 lemon | Zest of 1 orange | Icing sugar, for dusting |
| 1 tbsp bay leaf powder | Juice of 2 oranges | Salt |

### Method

Preheat the oven to 180°C/Gas Mark 4. To make the torta, beat the egg yolks and 150g of the sugar to a smooth cream. Mix in the lemon zest, bay leaf powder and almond extract, then add the ground almonds and combine well. In another bowl, beat the egg whites until stiff peaks form, then fold individual scoops into the almond mixture, until all the whites are used up and they are fully combined.

Grease a cake tin, then pour in the torta batter and transfer to the oven. Bake for 20 minutes until golden, then remove and let cool.

To make the syrup, heat the orange juice in a small pan with the orange zest, cardamom pods, the remaining sugar, olive oil and a pinch of salt. Bring to the boil, then reduce heat and let simmer until thick and glossy (about 20 minutes). Remove from the heat and discard the cardamom pods.

Turn out the cooled cake onto a plate, then dust with icing sugar (using a Santiago branding iron if you are feeling Spanish) and drizzle warm syrup over the top.

# KNOCK 'EM

# DOWN

No summer day at the beach passes without me cracking open a watermelon and stretching my jaws over a red wedge until the sticky sweet juice dribbles down my chest and mixes with sand. The bubblegum aroma brings back sunny memories of life when it was literally 'a beach' and when weekends seemed to never end.

The next hot afternoon (living in Barcelona means you don't have to wait long), I lugged home a giant striped green melon and set about creating a gazpacho that would compress the childlike pleasure of watermelon into a refined sweet red soup. I crushed the crisp flesh of the melon with tomatoes, fresh mint and lime juice, adding cucumber to cool the sweetness, then cracked pink peppercorns for a textural crunch.

Cool and sophisticated, this is the perfect way to enjoy watermelon when life forces you to grow up and engage in firm handshakes, an act that doesn't permit fingers covered in sticky pink juice.

# WATERMELON GAZPACHO

**15 MIN**

### Ingredients
½ watermelon, deseeded and roughly chopped
2 tomatoes, peeled and roughly chopped
½ cucumber, peeled and roughly chopped
Juice of 1 lime, plus wedges to serve
2 tbsp torn mint leaves
120g crème fraîche
Cracked black pepper

### Method
Blend the watermelon chunks with the tomatoes, cucumber, lime juice and mint until completely smooth, then season with pepper to taste. Transfer to the fridge to chill. Line the bottoms of your cocktail glasses with crème fraiche, then fill with gazpacho and top with pepper and a lime wedge. Slurp your way to a never-ending summer.

The modern world was all but banned in our house. Television was limited to the news, food was generally picked from our farm and swearing was a crime that warranted my mouth being vigorously scrubbed with yellow industrial soap (although the meaning of this action was lost with a mouth full of bubbles). But I managed to sneak the modern world in: pocket money went on refined sugar in the form of contraband McDonald's, candy was bought according to the best price-to-weight ratio, and chocolate milk was my own childhood experience of prohibition.

At age 14, anything that deviated from mainstream was a risk. With 'rock stars' as the fancy-dress theme at parties, I knew I had to choose Billie Joe Armstrong of punk band Green Day fame. I had the clothes, knew the words to all the songs and had my backpack filled with smuggled beer. Needing to add a crowning final touch, we agreed that my blonde locks simply would not do. My sisters convinced me to dye my hair. Getting artificial colourants past the powers that be was never going to happen, so we picked beetroots, dyed my hair a bright beetroot red, and the rest is history. I began the party in style, but ended with my head leaking red juice all through my friend's house, leaving some difficult questions to answer.

It's only now as I spend most of my life in the kitchen that I am grateful to my mother for her natural-at-all-costs approach. Her belief in nature was reinforced every time she set foot in the kitchen. Her food was simple, wholesome and naturally delicious. This was the food I grew up on, and the food you'll taste at my table once you get past the swipes and swirls. She had it right all along, but I've learnt to leave the vegetable dyes in the kitchen, where beetroot can bring life to creamed parsnip, carrots can give a delicious orange to hazelnut pesto, and saffron a golden-honey-yellow to fresh pears.

# SAFFRON POACHED PEARS
## WITH PINE NUT MASCARPONE

20 MIN

### Ingredients

720ml white wine

Peel of 1 lemon

1 cinnamon stick

A generous pinch of saffron threads

100g caster sugar

4 firm pears

4 tbsp pine nuts, toasted

115g mascarpone

Juice and zest of 1 orange

1 tsp rosewater

1 tbsp thyme, leaves

### Method

Put the wine, lemon peel, cinnamon stick, saffron threads and sugar in a saucepan and place over a medium heat. Bring to a simmer and allow to bubble away until reduced by half (about 20 minutes). Peel the pears leaving the stem attached and slice the bottom to create a stable base. Place the pears in the saucepan and reduce heat to a very slow simmer. Turn the pears occasionally in the liquid to ensure even cooking. After about 10 minutes and once the pears are tender, remove the pan from the heat and allow the pears to cool in the poaching liquid.

To make the pine nut mascarpone, grind the pine nuts in a mortar and pestle (reserving a few whole ones to decorate) until finely crushed. Combine the nuts with the mascarpone, orange zest and juice, and rosewater, then set aside. To serve, spread the mascarpone mixture over the plate, top with a pear and drizzle over a little poaching liquid. Finally, sprinkle with some of the reserved pine nuts.

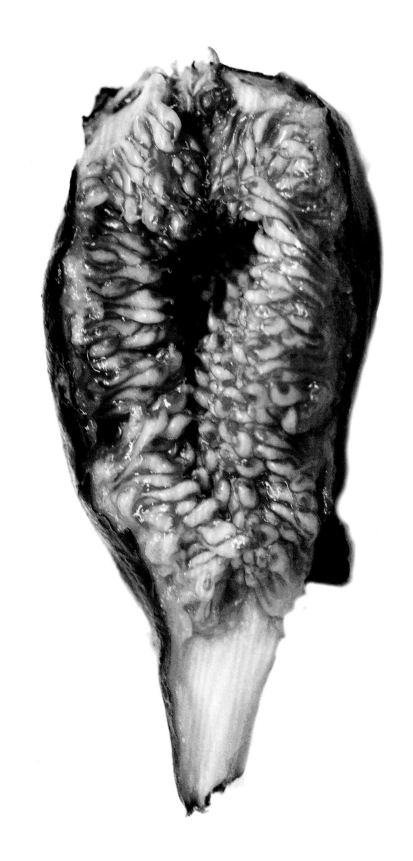

# A BIBLICAL FRUIT

## THAT MAKES YOU SWOON

# LET US

# PRAY

Religion lost its charm for me long ago, and not least because stories from the Bible were simply gastronomically incredulous. Who was the shameful author that chose an apple to represent sin, when the seductive fig would have caused Adam, and most of us, to do more than swoon at Eve's advances?

Figs ooze pheromones, and summer in Spain is filled with these plump biblical beauties. I was reminded of this every evening in Torredembarra as I crossed the bridge connecting the beach to my grandparents' house. Under the bridge grew a fig tree. Its leaves and ripe fruit acted as a filter through which the warm August air would waft, bringing with it an intoxicating scent that rivalled mistletoe in terms of allure.

171

# FRESH FIGS
## BAKED ON CRUNCHY WALNUT FRANGIPANE WITH A THYME SYRUP AND HONEY CREAM

**30 MIN**

## Ingredients

110g walnuts, toasted

50g plain white flour

50g brown sugar

1 tsp orange-blossom essence

2 eggs, beaten

1 tsp olive oil

240ml white wine

50g caster sugar

2 tbsp sherry

4 thyme sprigs

Zest of 1 lemon

120g whipping cream

2 tbsp honey

1 tbsp chopped mint leaves

10 fresh figs, sliced, plus extra to serve

Salt

## Method

Heat the oven to 180°C/Gas Mark 4. First, make the frangipane. Mix the walnuts, flour, sugar, orange-blossom essence, eggs and olive oil until a paste forms. Spread the frangipane evenly over a baking tray, then top with the fig slices. Sprinkle over a pinch of salt flakes and place in the oven. Bake for 15 minutes until the pastry is golden then remove and set aside to cool.

Meanwhile, make the syrup. Place the white wine, caster sugar, sherry, thyme sprigs and lemon zest in a small saucepan and set over a medium heat. Allow the sugar to dissolve, then reduce the heat and simmer until the liquid has become syrupy (about 20 minutes), then set aside.

To make the honey cream, whip the cream until it begins to thicken, then fold in the honey and mint.

Serve the figs drizzled with syrup and honey cream and additional fresh figs on the side.

My sisters and I began every holiday to Spain with manageable suitcases, but returned like pack-horses, struggling through strict Australian customs and their cute sniffer dogs. But the struggle was worth it. Unpacking in the January heat felt like Christmas all over again as we discovered heavy glass jars of addictively good Almendrina. This milky caramel made from almonds and sugar is for those who have graduated from the cute logos and outrageous health claims of Nutella. In Spain, Almendrina is used to flavour milk, dolloped over ice cream, on toast with a drizzle of olive oil or, like every one of us does in moments of Nutella weakness, eaten with a large spoon straight out of the jar.

# ALMENDRINA CHEESECAKE
## WITH PINEAPPLE CARAMELIZED
### IN CREMA NEGRITA

**45 MIN**

### Ingredients

50g of plain biscuits

60g walnuts

90g butter, melted

½ medium-sized pineapple, peeled, cored and flesh cubed

4 tbsp brown sugar

120ml crema negrita (or any other dark rum)

Juice of ½ a lime

500g mató (or ricotta)

50ml single cream

2 egg yolks

50g caster sugar

1 tsp vanilla essence

1 tbsp of Almendrina (honey will also work)

### Method

To make the base, crush the biscuits with the walnuts until you form a crumb, then stir through 40ml of the melted butter to form a paste. Spread the crumb mixture on the base of a cake tin and place in the fridge to chill while you make the other components.

To make the caramelized pineapple, add the cubed pineapple to a small pan with the remaining 50ml of butter and brown sugar and heat until the sugar has dissolved. Add the crema negrita, bring to a simmer and reduce until the syrup is beginning to caramelize (about 20 minutes). Add the lime juice and set aside.

Preheat the oven to 150°C/Gas Mark 2. To make the cheesecake, combine the mató (or ricotta) with the cream, egg yolks, sugar and vanilla essence until smooth. Remove the base from fridge and pour the cheesecake mixture over the top. Top with caramelized pineapple and transfer to the oven to bake for 15 minutes until set. Remove from the oven and set aside. Once cool, cut into wedges and drizzle over the Almendrina.

# MEMBRILLO AND FRESH CHEESE PASTRIES WITH LEMON SYRUP AND PISTACHIOS

**60 MIN**

On my childhood farm in Tasmania, quince trees sprouted their beautiful fruit every autumn and we would use every last one of them for poaching, jams, or marinating in orange juice and sharp white vinegar. The fruit would show up in crumbles, with ice cream or over a hot bowl of porridge in the morning, but I never truly understood the fruit that looked like a pear but took a lot more work to taste as good. It wasn't until my first trip to Spain when I tasted the delicious sweet tartness of *membrillo* (quince paste) paired with fresh cheese that this fruit began to make sense. *Membrillo* is a sure thing on every cheese plate and is savoury enough to hold its own in dishes of rabbit and rough chunks of pumpkin. Back home, I decided to recreate *membrillo* using the quinces that hung heavy on bare winter branches. With my mother's penchant for cutting every sugar measure in half, success demanded the addition of cinnamon and rosemary for a flavour that almost matched the Spanish tradition. In Spain, sticky-sweet pastries become more common the further south you travel, as the influence of the Moors begins to show up. Travel some 20,000km further south and you'll hit Tasmania and my homage to this famous Spanish flavour.

### Ingredients

Juice of 1 lemon

1 tbsp honey

4 tbsp butter

1 cinnamon stick

6 sheets of ready-rolled puff pastry

300g queso fresco, sliced thinly

100g membrillo (quince paste); see below

Zest of 1 orange

A sprinkling of caster sugar

60g pistachios, toasted

### Method

First, make the syrup. In a small saucepan, heat the lemon juice, honey and 1 tablespoon of butter, add the cinnamon stick, then reduce the sauce until glossy and thick, then set aside. Preheat the oven to 150°C/Gas Mark 2. Melt the remaining butter and brush it all over 3 sheets of puff pastry. Lay the 3 sheets on top of one another on a baking tray. Lay thin slices of the cheese on the pastry until completely covered, then top with the slices of membrillo and orange zest. Top with the other three sheets of pastry, brushing butter over each of them as before, then seal the pastry by pressing the bottom three layers together with the top three. Sprinkle the top with caster sugar and bake for 15 minutes until the pastry turns golden.

Reheat the syrup until it is runny, then drizzle it over the pastry and top with pistachios. Serve with hot mint tea or a sweet Muscat wine.

# MEMBRILLO

### Ingredients

4 quinces, peeled, cored and roughly chopped

1 vanilla pod, split

1 rosemary sprig

1 cinnamon stick

Peel and juice of ½ lemon

750g raw sugar

### Method

Place the quince pieces in a large pan and cover with water. Add the vanilla pod, rosemary, cinnamon and lemon peel. Set over a high heat and bring to a boil, then reduce the heat to a simmer, cover the pan and leave to cook for 30 minutes until tender. Strain the quince and discard the vanilla pod, rosemary and cinnamon stick, but keep the lemon peel. Purée the quince pieces in a food processor until smooth, then transfer to a saucepan, measuring the amount of purée as you go. For every 225g of purée, add 150g of sugar. Put the quince pan over a medium heat, and stir with a wooden spoon until the sugar has completely dissolved. Add the lemon juice and continue to cook over a low heat, stirring occasionally, for at least an hour until the quince paste has thickened and turns a dark pink–orange (about 1 hour).

Preheat the oven to 100°C/Gas Mark ½, then turn off. Line a baking tray with greased baking paper. Pour the quince paste over the paper, spreading it evenly with a knife. Place the baking tray in the still-warm oven for about an hour to allow the quince to dry, then remove and let cool. Remove the paste from the tray and cut it into squares, then store it in the fridge where it will keep for several months.

# SORBET

Ice cream is an evergreen, an all-year-rounder, but, even in the heat of Spanish summer, it sometimes fails to take the edge off, melting as quickly as it's scooped. This is not the case with sorbet, which offers a white-hot icy coldness that can counter the midday sun. There are no tricks – it's water, sugar, flavour and a freezer, and this clarity is exactly what I'm looking for in the middle of summer. Ice-cream is made to be licked and slurped – and can even be comforting in the depths of winter, while sorbet is seasonal and limited to the peak of summer when carved curls of sweet ice push you closer and closer towards that painfully good 'brain freeze'.

## 3 HR

No bee ever attacked a delicate petal only to have their hard labour strangled into moulded yellow plastic tubes. The bears got it right all along; honey with its intoxicating sweetness deserves to be uncontrollably scooped from jars and licked from sticky paws. In Spain, honey comes in as many flavours as its mountains have flowers. On a road trip inland, we came across a couple of small, shy children manning a table covered in mismatched jars: dark-chestnut, almost black, honey; the beautifully sweet rosemary honey; and my favourite, the herbaceous heather honey. There was nothing packaged about the operation, with prices scrawled on the sticky jars and flecks of wax and comb mixed through the golden liquid. This was the honey that bees lived for – raw and natural with a violent sweetness that only the mountains of Catalonia can produce.

# HONEY AND THYME

### Ingredients

8 thyme sprigs
340g honey
3 tbsp apple cider vinegar

2 tbsp thyme flowers
Olive oil
Zest of 1 orange

### Method

Pour 480ml of boiling water into a bowl. Add 4 whole thyme sprigs and leave to infuse. Once the water has cooled, strain it through a sieve into a separate bowl. Add the honey and stir until it has dissolved. Then, add the vinegar. Pour the mixture into an ice-cream maker and churn until almost frozen, then transfer to the freezer for at least 4 hours to harden up, stirring it every 30 minutes. Heat a lug of olive oil in a small frying pan over a high heat. Pick the leaves off the remaining 4 thyme sprigs and fry until crispy. To serve, scoop the sorbet into a bowl, then sprinkle with crispy thyme leaves, thyme flowers and orange zest.

# CINNAMON AND COCOA

The Bible has always been a collection of interesting and sometimes inspiring stories, but my real guide has been a small, unassuming book called the *The Flavour Thesaurus* by Niki Segnit. Packed with weird and wonderful combinations, this book is my go-to reference when vermouth doesn't provide the necessary inspiration. Cinnamon and cocoa is comforting and at the same time intoxicating and is perfect in a crisp, icy sorbet.

### Ingredients

| | | | |
|---|---|---|---|
| 200g raw sugar | 1 tsp cinnamon powder | 30ml crème de cacao | and halved |
| 50g cocoa powder | 1 cinnamon stick | 50g hazelnuts, toasted | A pinch of salt |

### Method

Put the sugar, cocoa, cinnamon powder, salt and cinnamon stick in a large pan with 500ml of water. Slowly bring to the boil, stirring, until the sugar has completely dissolved. Leave to boil for 5 minutes, then remove from the heat. Leave to cool, remove the cinnamon stick and transfer to the fridge to chill until cold. Once cold, pour the mixture into a container and freeze for at least 4 hours, stirring it every 30 minutes. Remove the sorbet from the freezer and transfer to a food processor or blender, whizz to break up until smooth, then put the sorbet back in the container and refreeze for a further 1 hour. To serve, scoop the sorbet into individual bowls, then top with a drizzle of the crème de cacao and sprinkle over the hazelnuts.

# STRAWBERRY AND ROSEMARY

Every berry has a partner in crime. I like anise with raspberries, cumin with blueberries, orange peel with black berries, and rosemary with the common but still exquisite strawberry.

### Ingredients

| | |
|---|---|
| 65g caster sugar | 1 tbsp lemon juice |
| 2 tbsp rosemary leaves | 50g desiccated coconut, toasted |
| 500g strawberries | |

### Method

Put the sugar in a small saucepan with 80ml of water. Add the rosemary and place on a low heat. Bring the mixture to the boil for 1 minute, then remove from heat. Strain the liquid through a sieve into a container and transfer to the fridge to chill until cold. Purée the strawberries in a food processor or blender, then transfer to a large bowl and add the lemon juice. Chill in the refrigerator for at least 4 hours, stirring every 30 minutes. Combine the chilled sugar mixture and strawberry purée and pour into an ice-cream machine. Churn until soft set, then transfer to the freezer to harden. Serve in bowls with sprinkled coconut over the top.

# BABIES
# DRINK FROM THE BREAST
# CHEFS
# DRINK FROM THE BOTTLE

*Leche merengada* is an intoxicating combination of milk, cinnamon, lemon and sugar and a truly Spanish flavour. Thankfully, it comes in a several different forms: as a sweet, milky drink sold in giant bottles at supermarkets; chilled and sold in takeaway cups by street vendors; and scooped as ice cream during the summer. But it was a sweet, milky rice pudding that served as my first introduction to the flavour combination. Papa Serra would finish most meals with this dessert as we sat around the table mingling conversations in Catalan, German, Spanish and English (things are complicated in my family).

I never paid much attention to what was being said. Instead, I watched Papa Serra, in his late eighties at this stage, calmly spoon up his milky rice pudding without saying much and staring into the distance. My memories of him aren't as complete as I wish they were; black-and-white photographs count for only so much. But the photos, together with the stories, give me a sense of the man who became, and still is, my strongest connection with Catalonia.

# LECHE MERENGADA
## ICE CREAM

**3 HR**

### Ingredients

1 litre milk
250g caster sugar
Peel of 1 lemon
1 cinnamon stick
3 egg whites
Ground cinnamon, for dusting
85g flaked almonds, toasted
Salt

### Method

Put the milk, 150g of the sugar, the lemon peel and the cinnamon stick in a medium saucepan over a medium heat and simmer until the sugar has completely dissolved. Remove from the heat, allow to cool, then strain into a container. Put the lid on the container and freeze, stirring occasionally until the mixture becomes slushy. When it has almost set, beat the egg whites with a pinch of salt until foamy. Gradually add the remaining sugar, continuing to whisk throughout, until stiff peaks form. Fold the meringue into the milky slush, then return to the freezer for another 10 minutes until solid. Serve with a dusting of cinnamon and a sprinkling of flaked almonds.

183

# FALL IN LOVE
## OR
## FALL IN
# CHOCOLATE
## IT'S KIND OF THE SAME THING

Chocolate transcends classification in the food pyramid; it seems more at home on the bedroom dresser alongside aftershave, gold watches, silk ties and the good life. Every dark square has only ever satisfied one human need: pleasure. Chocolate should be neither chewed nor chomped. Neither gnawed nor gulped. And definitely not munched or masticated. It must be licked, savoured, relished and adored. It must be loved.

I grew up in Australia where chocolate was milky and bland (thank you Cadbury and your 23% cocoa solids). And while Spanish chocolates sent every year from gastronomically minded grandparents made life a little smoother Down Under, the world of the dark bean was uninteresting and I spent my meagre pocket money on gob stoppers and Wizz Fizz (Google both for a visual of 90s childhood heaven). And then I met Lindt. Like my coffee, I now take my chocolate strong and black – hold the milk and sugar. I began with the basic milk chocolate (43% cocoa solids), advanced to 55%, then easily stepped up to 70%. I became adventurous with the now mainstream 85%, and then, in a blackening spiral, discovered their 99% gold label and chocolate ecstasy. Fall in love, or fall in chocolate, because as someone more poetic than me once said, 'It's kind of the same thing'.

# OLIVE OIL CHOCOLATE MOUSSE
## WITH SUMAC STRAWBERRIES, ROSEMARY CRUNCH AND ORANGE MASCARPONE

**30 MIN**

### Ingredients

100g strawberries, pitted and halved

1 tbsp sumac

Juice of 1 lemon

60g walnuts, toasted

2 tbsp of rosemary, finely chopped

1 tbsp brown sugar

2 tbsp mascarpone

Zest of 1 orange

1 tsp cinnamon

100g dark chocolate (at least 70% cocoa)

55ml extra-virgin olive oil

300ml whipping cream

Salt

### Method

Toss the strawberries with the sumac and lemon juice and set aside. To make the rosemary crunch, put the walnuts, rosemary and brown sugar into a blender and pulse until crumbly, then set aside. Combine the mascarpone with the orange zest and cinnamon and beat until smooth, then set aside.

Now, make the mousse. Melt the dark chocolate in a double boiler, then reduce the heat and gently stir in the olive oil and the salt. Take the bowl off the heat and allow the chocolate mixture to cool. In a separate bowl, whip the cream until it forms soft peaks, then gently fold the chocolate into the cream until fully combined. Spoon the mousse into individual bowls, then top with the strawberries and mascarpone mixture and sprinkle over the rosemary crunch.

# DRINKS
## SUPERHEROES STAY HYDRATED

# CAFÉ CON HIELO

Summer doesn't mean humans don't need caffeine. On the contrary, the extent of partying during the summer demands a higher dosage than usual. But a warm, milky cup of *café con leche* or short hot shot of espresso is too much when the Mediterranean sun is flexing its warm muscles. The solution is *café con hielo*, a beautiful concept where a glass of ice is served with a shot of espresso. In a flowing motion, you tip the hot black coffee over the ice, which cracks on contact and immediately transforms the drink into one you can enjoy for just as long as it takes for the ice to melt.

*Horchata* is my Spanish milkshake of choice. Native to Valencia, the Spanish version of this Latin American tradition is made using ground tigernuts (*xufas*) but, depending on where in Latin America you are, might also be based around ground almonds, sesame seeds, rice or barley, mixed with water and sugar, then chilled. The creamy liquid is refreshing and sweet and will lift you above the hot Spanish afternoons that sometimes appear to have no end. You can buy *horchata* in plastic bottles at supermarkets, but it is worth seeking out a traditional bar, where big cardboard cups are filled to the brim and then dusted with cinnamon. There is a place in the world for a desperate bottle of iced coffee from the gas station, a strawberry thickshake from McDonald's, and even the creamy Coke spider, but these days I save my straw for *horchata*.

# HORCHATA

### Ingredients

100g horchata nuts (known as *xufas* or *chufas* throughout Spain)
Ground cinnamon, for dusting
1 or 2 cinnamon sticks, to serve (optional)

### Method

Soak the horchata nuts in water (use a ratio of 100g horchata nuts for every 70ml of water) for two days in the fridge to soften the nuts, then blend the nuts and soaking water together until smooth. Strain through a fine sieve, then blend again with additional water as required to reach a milky consistency. If you have a sweet tooth, add sugar to taste. Serve chilled over ice and dusted with cinnamon. For added authenticity use a cinnamon quill as an inefficient but definitely authentic straw.

# VICHY

I like clean flavours and you can't get much cleaner than the naturally salty Vichy mineral water. Incredibly mineralized, Vichy is the water of choice in Catalonia with good reason. The flavour pairs perfectly with plates of olives, salty white anchovies or a simple sandwich of *jamón* and manchego, without washing out your palate like the inferior brands that are thirst-quenching but bland. It's for the gourmand, and once you check its price-tag outside of Spain, you'll agree it must be holy water.

Cava makes every day special. The bottles of bubbly follow the same labelling principles as Champagne and can only be called cava if the grapes were grown in a specific designated region of Spain. But that is where the similarities end. There is nothing refined about how Spaniards celebrate, and cava, with its larger bubbles, is for throwing back in joyful gulps, not sipping in measured celebration.

# CAVA

### Ingredients
Cava, chilled
50g strawberries, thinly sliced
1 tbsp white sugar
2–3 lemon wedges

### Method
Preheat an oven to its lowest setting. Place the sliced strawberries onto baking paper and transfer to the oven for 2–3 hours or until dry. Take the strawberry slices out of the oven and transfer to the freezer for 10 minutes to freeze out the remaining moisture. Put the strawberry slices in a blender together with the sugar and whizz until you have a fine power. Tip the powder onto a plate. Rim each cava glass with lemon juice, then dip the rim in the strawberry powder. Turn the glasses upright again and fill with chilled cava.

It's all in the pour with Asturian cider. I tried it for the first time at a rocking bar in Gràcia, one of Barcelona's coolest neighbourhoods and my home for several years. *Pintxos*, the entrance to which was heralded by a loud bell, arrived fresh from the kitchen every 5 minutes before being seized upon by all within earshot. The food was good, but the cider was better. What makes Asturian cider so special is the pouring technique drinkers must first master, with the cider poured from great heights before splashing and crashing into the glass below. The special technique to *escanciar* (pour) the cider serves as a visual spectacle, but also aerates the cider and improves its flavour. Watch the barman the first time before trying to imitate this inevitably messy but definitely recommended local custom.

# ASTURIAN APPLE CIDER

### Ingredients
A bottle of chilled Asturian cider

### Method
Hold the bottle by its neck in one hand and hold a glass by its base and on a slight tilt with the other hand. Begin pouring at chest level, then slowly separate your hands while continuing to pour until your hands are as far apart as possible. Fill your glass (hopefully not the rest of the bar) and enjoy this crisp tangy beverage.

One of the most distinctive components of Spanish life is the locals' relationship with alcohol. No doubt Spaniards enjoy alcohol, but there is a calmness to drinking in Spain that Anglo cultures lack. A Spanish gathering won't simply focus on eating, drinking, talking or dancing, but will require participants to master a combination of the four activities; quite distinct from my experience in Australia, London, the US, and even Sweden, where you meet to focus on accomplishing just one of these activities at a time. In Spain, I find so much pleasure in meeting up with friends for tapas and a glass of something, before walking to another bar and repeating. The Clara for me typifies drinking culture. Without needing to prove itself in a pint glass, a beer is pulled to three quarters full before some lemon squash is added. It makes for a flavour combination that puts the shandy to shame and means that the bright atmosphere goes from street to club and back again, with police needed only to keep happy voices and wide smiles in check.

# CLARA

### Ingredients
Spanish beer (Moritz is my favourite)
Lemon squash (Trina in Spain, Lift and Solo everywhere else)

### Method
Fill a chilled glass ⅓ full with lemon squash, then fill to the brim with beer. Adjust the ratio depending on your taste. And remember to use a small glass so every sip right down to the last gulp is ice cold.

Sangria can be as simple as a bottle of wine, some fruit, some soda water and some sugar, but you can also enter gourmet territory with the addition of cinnamon sticks or a sprig of rosemary. Throwing a party to mark the end of 2009, our house decided that chilled jugs of sangria would be the perfect antidote to melting temperatures of 40°C. The party began timidly enough, but several hours later, the deep bowl of sangria that my housemate and I had lovingly prepared was close to empty. Lacking bottles of the cheap sangria-destined wine, and with the festivities somewhat clouding our judgement, we made a decision to raid our carefully guarded collection of bottles that should have been destined for a special dinner party. But parties wait for no one and the special occasion was now. We mixed bottles of reserve (some with 90s' vintage) into another heaving cauldron of sangria and returned to face the thirsty revellers. With smiles back on everyone's faces, we shared a congratulatory moment of satisfaction, not fully cognisant of what had just taken place. The next morning during clean-up, the brutal reality was there for all to see. But it was worth it, and if I learned any lessons that night, it is first that you can never have enough sangria, and second that you should never make important decisions midway through a party.

# SANGRIA

### Ingredients

1 orange, halved and sliced

50g strawberries, pitted and quartered

1 peach, stoned and cut into chunks

1 bunch rosemary

50g caster sugar

60ml lime juice

750ml bottle of light, dry red wine (Granache or Pinot Noir is perfect)

100ml white rum

500ml bottle of soda water

### Method

Fill a large glass jug with the fruit (feel free to add more or less of your favourite) and the rosemary, then add the sugar, lime juice, red wine and white rum and stir until the sugar has dissolved. Top with soda water and transfer to the fridge to chill and to give the fruit time to absorb the alcohol. Serve in chilled glasses over ice and, if sangria is your party centrepiece, feel free to add more white rum to give the red liquid, and your party, a certain edge.

When I was growing up, every birthday in my family began with my father's homemade buttery croissants and my mother's Spanish hot chocolate – presents were immaterial and pushed aside in favour of that heady breakfast. I somehow went almost a decade as an adult without hot chocolate and it wasn't until I was in Madrid one winter that I fell for the familiar taste again. A friend took me to an old *chocolatería* as the sun set and the desert-like chill descended on the city. Crunchy *churros*, dusted in sugar and cinnamon were brought to the table, along with two big mugs of liquid chocolate. Sitting at that café in Madrid was a long way from the birthday traditions of my childhood, but the taste was just as familiar.

# SPANISH HOT CHOCOLATE

### Ingredients
100g dark chocolate (at least 70% cocoa), roughly chopped
100ml milk

### Method
Pour the milk into a small saucepan and set over a low heat. Slowly heat the milk, whisking continuously, until it begins to simmer. Add the chopped chocolate and continue to whisk until the chocolate has melted and the liquid is thick and dark. Remove from the heat. Don't worry if you think it's too bitter, the sweetness of flaky croissants or crunchy fried pastries like churros act as the perfect foil.

My hydration of choice in Barcelona is black vermouth. I fell for the fortified black *vermut* in a big way and now tend give in to its bitter allure throughout the entire day (not just at '*la hora de vermut*' before lunch, as locals advise). At the dinner parties I host on my rooftop, vermouth remains the lubricant by which guests from all over the world start nights as awkward strangers, but finish as best of friends. Vermouth is my go-to when I need a boost of creativity to reflect on life in and out of the kitchen. In fact, I owe a lot of this book and my life in Barcelona to this magical dark joy.

# VERMOUTH

### Ingredients
1 orange, sliced into thin wedges
100ml vermouth (not the white or red martini vermouth, but black homemade vermouth)
3 green Sevillana olives
Soda water, to serve

### Method
Put some ice cubes and a thin wedge of orange in a glass, then cover in vermouth. Spear a toothpick with a few olives and set on the glass to serve. Serve with soda water on the side. Add a plate of olives and crisps and you will get a bit closer to understanding why Spain has life sorted.

ROBINSON

First published in Great Britain in 2017 by Robinson

1 3 5 7 9 10 8 6 4 2

Photography by Aldo Chacon

Design by Jouk Inthesky

A CIP catalogue record for this book
is available from the British Library.

ISBN 978-1-47214-026-5

Printed and bound in China

Robinson
An imprint of
Little, Brown Book Group
Carmelite House
50 Victoria Embankment
London EC4Y 0DZ

An Hachette UK Company
www.hachette.co.uk

www.littlebrown.co.uk